D0229689

are you Rich?

Katherine Higgins

CHAMELEON

To mummy, for her endless help, patience & encouragement

designed by: Linda Baritski at Generation

First published in Great Britain in 1999 by Chameleon Books
76 Dean Street, London, W1V 5HA

Copyright © Katherine Higgins 1999

All rights reserved. This book is sold subject to the condition that it may not be reproduced, stored in a retrieval system, or transmitted in any form or by any means, electronic, mechanical, photocopying, recording or otherwise, without the publisher's prior consent

CIP data for this title is available from the British Library
ISBN 0 233 99211 1

Origination by Digicol Link, London

Printed by Jarrold Book Printing

The prices indicated are intended as a guide only and summarise the current market trends. There are many factors such as condition that will affect the value of any collectable and neither the author nor publisher accept any liability for any financial or other loss incurred by reliance placed on the information contained in *Are You Rich?*

HUNDREDS OF HOUSHOLD ITEMS THAT CAN MAKE YOU A FORTUNE

are you Rich?

IN THE
Kitchen

in the kitchen

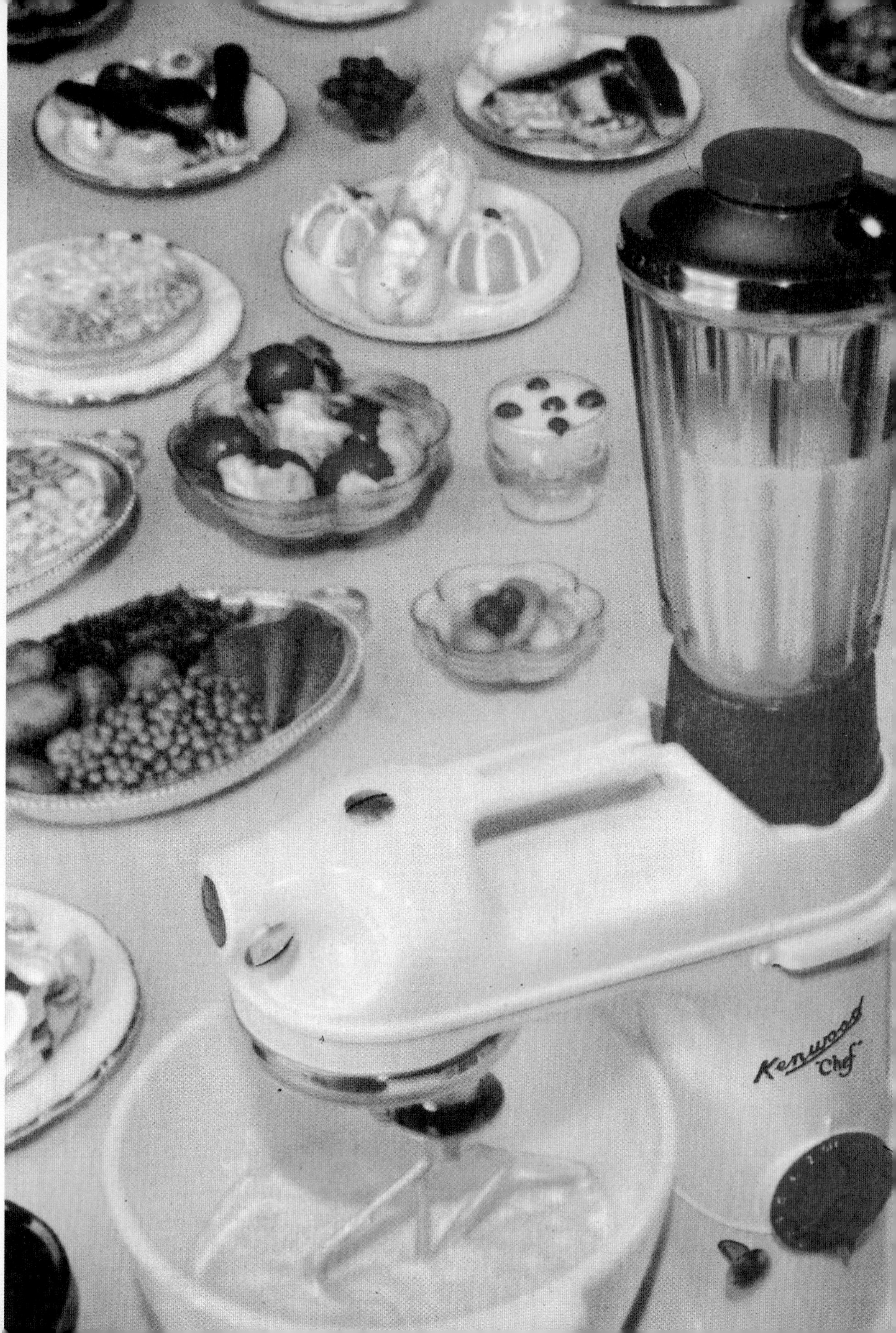

When the fifties dawned so did modern-style living. The kitchen, a room traditionally tucked away at the back of the house, became a Formica-bright, clean-at-a-wipe focal point in most homes. Cooking in isolation was banished and a new breed of designers and architects (hotfoot from styling Britain's booming 'New Towns') brought the busy housewife face to face with the rest of her family in American-style 'kitchen/diners'.

Ergonomic studies like the 1953 Cornell Report advocated 'work centres' and 'work triangles' in the kitchen, to help with the daily grind of cooking chores. But most domestic assistance in the fifties came from the mass of new labour saving appliances, unveiled at the annual *Daily Mail* Ideal Home Exhibition. Once these gadgets were mastered it was time to experiment. For those with a taste for 'modern' cookery, in the shape of Elizabeth David's Mediterranean recipes, an array of previously unheard of ingredients and kitchen utensils were now available.

In the sixties, kitchen gadgets became mass-market affordable, thanks to easy-pay hire-purchase schemes. By 1965 the number of families owning vacuum cleaners and washing machines, for instance, had doubled in comparison with the previous decade.

Modular veneered kitchen units were a fashionable way of furnishing a sixties kitchen and Hygena's 'System 70'(launched in 1963) championed an all-new 'built-in' concept. It wasn't long before homes bristled with built-in refrigerators, swivel shelves, a split-level oven and hob, inset sinks and a waste disposal unit. Lashings of stainless steel accessories and all-in-one cookware, available from the newly opened Habitat store (1964).

The kitchen of the seventies was a walk-through eating/dining affair – a place where the housewife could prepare supper and still remain in contact with her family and friends. Only this time, popular cookery connoisseur 'The Galloping Gourmet' (Graham Kerr), stressed the importance of a 'road block' serving centre to divide the two areas, and a less-fitted approach to units with the accent on discreet styling.

The seventies was the first real DIY decade and Crown demonstrated their new ready-pasted vinyl wallpapers in bold floral patterns in 1972. They were 'wipe down and tough for the kitchen' and fitted well with QA (quick assembly) flat-pack units. Flow-through decoration was a must and few gadgets, saucepans, oven-to-tableware or storage jars from this decade escaped without some sort of florid pattern. Time saving was still on the agenda, and the biggest move in this direction came from the world's first domestic food processor, the mighty Magimix, which saved on utensils and the washing up!

Ten years on, the kitchen was even more of a multi-activity space – an emotional nerve centre for the home and a room for cooking, eating and relaxing in. Eighties technology moved modern appliances forward and advertisers were quick to stress the advantages of 'in-built micro-chip technology'. Although America first saw microwave ovens in the mid-fifties, by the eighties they were commonplace in most British kitchens, putting plastic utensils and containers above traditional ceramic and stainless steel in the cook's hierarchy. Clean, clinical white was the over-riding colour in most kitchens and wipe-down simulated marble work surfaces were kept uncluttered, with the exception of a smattering of the best Alessi or Bodum design.

By the early nineties the ground rules for today's kitchen design were set. It's taken five decades to evolve into a family room that's acceptable for entertaining guests too. Perhaps that's why true nineties cooks take pains to strategically display their gadgets and gizmos. As a wave of retro American style has crept into most appliance design, the designs may look back a few decades, but materials remain distinctly nineties.

in the kitchen

CONA COFFEE

For those in tune with fifties youth culture and the mass of trendy coffee bars that sprang up spreading the Italian love of freshly brewed coffee, a Cona coffee machine was a must. Not only slickly styled and sculptural, the Cona was also practical thanks to its clear borosilicate (like Pyrex) heatproof glass which enabled you to see the brewing in front of your eyes! An early version, the Rex, which looked a little like this fifties model, was the work of British graphic artist Abram Games (1914-97) – known for the Festival of Britain symbol – who was persuaded by Cona's owner to have a go at three-dimensional design. After a showing at the Festival of Britain in 1951 his design sparked mass production and more advanced models like this appeared. If you're lucky enough to find a Cona 'Rex', check the glass bowls are original – they'll be marked 'Rex'. However, this mass produced version is still sought after for its flamboyant fifties style.

£300+ (Cona Rex) £25+ (mass market Cona)

FORMICA

Fifties kitchens were incomplete without a colourful, wipe-down table. The 'wonder' laminated plastic, Formica, which quickly replaced enamel in the kitchen, tops this one. It hailed from the States where two entrepreneurs,

Herbert Faber and Daniel J. O'Conor, who founded the Formica Corporation in 1913, had discovered how to make a tough, heat-resistant covering from thermal-set resin-impregnated paper. In 1947 Formica hit Britain with its range of 'gay' colours and its classic simulated textile surface. No need for clumsy tablecloths to hide these 'jewel-bright, clean-at-a-wipe' tabletops! In powder-blue with splayed 'spider' legs this table, and its matching plastic-covered chairs, are typically fifties. But a lack of any maker's mark explains its reasonable price. Do watch out for chipping and scratching on the surface as it will reduce value.
£70-90

In an age of appliances, owning the latest model was vital. For those who had lost their servants these handy electrical gadgets would do '101 jobs in the kitchen for the "modern" housewife'. The first all-British mixer, the Kenwood A200, appeared in 1948 but was swiftly updated to the aptly named Kenwood Electric 'Chef', priced at a hefty £19 10s 10d. For a few shillings extra, a range of ten 'gay colour' plastic accessories was available, meaning the basic white model could be transformed to tone in with any kitchen scheme. This one still has its 'ultra-smart' black nose cap, cover cap and control switch ('sunshine yellow', green, 'gay red' and blue were also on offer). For those who couldn't make up their mind, there was always an in-store demonstration by the Kenwood girl! **£50-60**

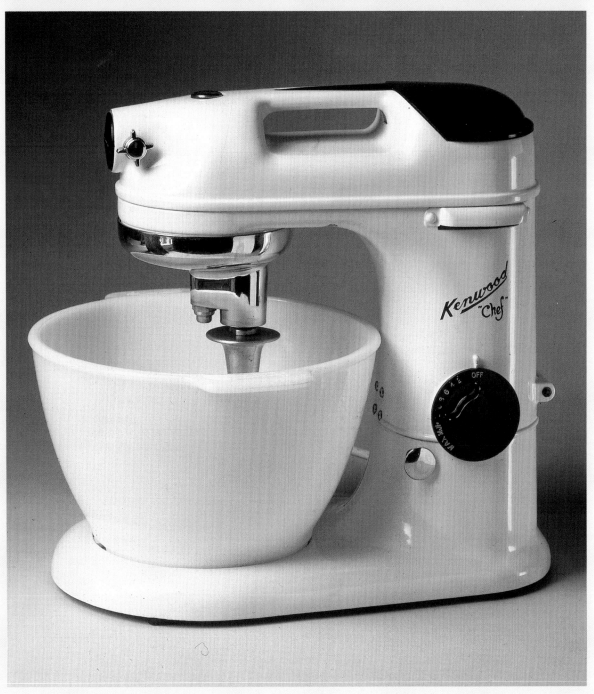

in the kitchen

These recipe pamphlets were a subtle way of building brand loyalty. With food rationing still in force in the early fifties, manufacturers were seen as benevolent with their practical helpful hints on how to make 'economical shortbread'. But they were paving the way for the end of rationing when the market would prove far more competitive and a little customer loyalty would count! Woe betide those who switched brands, as Stork Margarine's Cookery Service leaflet pointed out: 'in this book we tell you why you should follow our instructions and what will happen if you don't'! **£1.50-4.50 each**

The Sunbeam Mixmaster brought American style to the British kitchen when it first appeared in Britain in 1955. Unlike the Kenwood Chef the top could be detached and used as a portable hand mixer, although it was far from light! Success was virtually guaranteed with the Mixmaster's 'bowl-fit beaters' – curved to the contours of the bowl. Look out for the elusive white and chrome, pink and white and yellow and white two-tone versions. **£65**

If making it the real way was too much trouble then Nestlé's, (est. 1867) Nescafé instant coffee was the ideal alternative. From 1950 to 1959 sales of the soluble coffee powder, first seen on the market in 1937, tripled. Contemporary advertisements, showing families gathered around their new TV sets, championed the fact that Nescafé was 'so quick to make, you don't miss a thing'. When grocery chain Sainsbury's opened their first self-service store in 1950 distinctly branded products like this stood out on the shelves, vital to consumers who could at last choose for themselves. **£6**

The Queen's Coronation in 1953 spawned a host of souvenirs. One rarity (only if it's in mint condition) that found its way into the kitchen is this vacuum flask by royal warrant holders Thermos Limited (founded 1907). It even has its original paper wrapper to protect the stopper. Scratched and dented it would be worth £10 but in this A1 condition it's valued at far more. **£60**

This 'gingham' kitchen wall clock, made by T.G. Green (founded 1864) of blue and white Cornish ware fame, was said to be 'just right for modern living'. The colourful checked pattern appeared around 1954 in two colours, maroon and suede green, although pottery clocks like these were also made in a blue check. T.G. Green cleverly teamed up with a renowned electrical firm, Smiths, to make a clock that not only looked good but also smacked of reliability. As clocks are hard to find today they are worth more than the matching gingham jugs, bowls and teacups. **£40-60**

TASTY TREATS

In an age of canapés and cocktail nibbles – no cook could do without Nutbrown's (est. 1927) party biscuit cutters. Thanks to Constance Spry's famous *Cookery Book* (1956) the housewife could learn how to entertain with flair and prepare a selection of 'cocktail savouries'. Each cutter was precisely sized and came in suitably varied modern shapes. Today, Japanese collectors snap up most kitchenware like this, providing it is complete and in good condition.
£10-15

Convenient, easy to use and most importantly controllable on those new synthetic fibres like ICI's Terylene and British Celanese's acetate rayons, steam irons were a bonus for the busy housewife. They first appeared in the thirties but their primitive features were all but 'ironed out' two decades on. This one from 1953, by Hoover (founded 1908), was one of the first to be seen in Britain.
£10 (boxed)

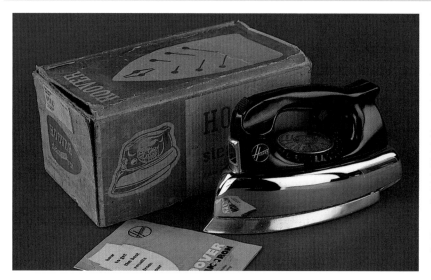

COLOURED PYREX

As colour touched almost every aspect of fifties living also it influenced American firm Corning's Pyrex designs. Tinted 'opal ware' in 'cheery' pink, turquoise, 'sunny yellow', 'gay red' and avocado soon found a loyal following. As the adverts said, these were 'decorator colours designed to harmonize with modern or traditional table settings'. American housewives were the first to see colour when Pyrex's vivid bowl sets hit their stores in 1947. But Britain was swift to follow thanks to licensed Pyrex manufacturer James A. Jobling & Co (who produced Pyrex in Sunderland from 1922). From 1951 Milner Gray and Kenneth Lamble from the Design Research Unit helped Jobling to style their new-look Pyrex dishes including these distinctive 'jockey cap' soup bowls. And most kitchens at one stage had a few pieces from Jobling's 'Easy Grip' casserole range (launched 1953), which went on to win a Design Award. Patterns like the classic 'Snowflake' appeared towards the end of the decade. Pyrex in all forms is avidly collected in the States but it's still early days here so buy while you can! Check the marks to establish true Jobling pieces; the distinctive 'Pyrex' on a banner with a crown above was Gray's mark and was first seen in 1953, which should help with dating. **£4.50 ('Snowflake' jockey cap bowls) £18 ('Snowflake' covered vegetable dish)**

Branded 'the cleaner that walks on air', the Hoover Constellation was a serious status symbol when it first came out in 1956. Its modern space age design, equally advanced hovercraft-style operation (available for models made from 1957) and use of *the* latest plastics technology, made it the vacuum cleaner to own – providing you had a smooth carpet. Anything too thick and it was more a case of pulling than gliding! Sales were so good on both sides of the Atlantic, due to Hoover's door to door demonstrating, that British Pop artist Richard Hamilton (b.1922) parodied Hoover's status-building Constellation along with other household gadgets in his 1956 collage 'Just what is it that makes today's home so different, so appealing?' **£50+ (in good condition)**

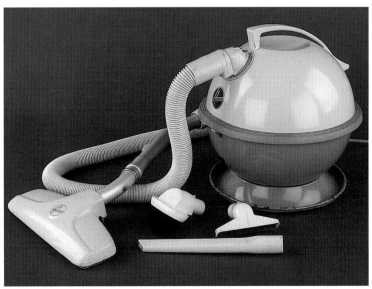

For purity of design the Kitchen Machine (sold as the Magicmaid in Britain) designed by Gerd Alfred Muller (1932-91) and made by German manufacturers Braun (est. 1921) in 1957 was the ultimate. It was superbly functional with indentations in the edge of the bowl, so mixing those sponge cakes was a far more controlled affair that made you a 'wizard in your own kitchen'. Its streamlined looks set the ground rules for German appliance design and its success is measured by the fact that it remained in production for more than 25 years. Check the serial number and styling to search for early models. Mint condition is vital and it helps if you can find the original box, instruction leaflet and 112-page recipe book sold with it. **£100-120**

The world's first automatic electric kettle, the K1, launched by Russell Hobbs in 1955, could hardly have come from anywhere else but Britain (a nation of confirmed tea drinkers!). This is the firm's improved K2 model, which appeared in 1959, still with its revolutionary 'forgettable' function. If you happened to get too engrossed in your newly purchased TV set, a vapour-controlled cut-out in the handle automatically switched off the current when the water boiled (handy and economical too!). Not to be confused with the not so collectable matt stainless steel versions of the 1960s and later. **£35-40**

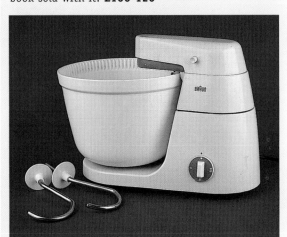

the SiXties

in the kitchen

This striking re-design of Kenwood's Chef in 1960 by Kenneth Grange (b.1929) brought a much-loved kitchen aid up to date. Its sleek lines recalled the simplicity of Braun's earlier 'Kitchen Machine'. But after just four days of designing, Grange came up with a totally individual mixer. He balanced ease of use (new click-in, click-out attachments) and mechanical power with the new Kenwood 'sheer look'. The two-tone blue and white plastic body not only disguised the Chef's overall mass but somehow gave it a personality too. Priced at £28 17s 6d – the equivalent of a week's income, the redesigned Chef wasn't cheap, but you could pay in weekly instalments. Kenwood's founder, Kenneth Wood, used his profits to fund an instant repair service for customers countrywide. In the rare event of the Chef not functioning properly a Kenwood man-in-a-van would arrive to fix it in your home – a service that helped to seal customer loyalty. No wonder *Good Housekeeping* magazine voted the Kenwood Chef, 'the British housewife's all-time favourite kitchen appliance'. Originals like this one, in pristine condition with all the attachments, are hard to find today. **£40-50**

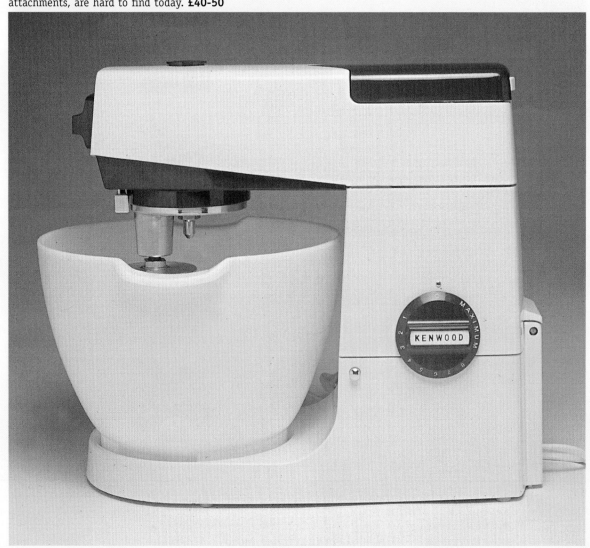

Stainless steel was hardly new in the 1960s but it was considered an industrial material, rather than anything suitable for the home. All that changed when British firms like Viners and J & J Wiggin's, Old Hall, took a lead from Scandinavia and made stainless steel fashionable. If you wanted an ultra-smart look in 1962 then this stainless steel teaset was it. Designed by silversmith Robert Welch (b.1929) for Old Hall's 'Alveston Range' it was sophisticated, stylish and long lasting. And the poor conductivity of stainless steel meant it kept liquids hot too. The price of £24 19s 6d (from Heal's) wasn't exactly cheap but the teaset did go on to win a Design Centre Award in 1965 and as a result spawned a host of cheaper copies. **£200+**

Oven-to-table ware was ideal for space saving and great for time saving when it came to the dreaded washing up! Jobling's 'Pyrosil Ware' was on hand to help you 'prepare and serve' with the added bonus that it cut your cooking costs down too. It was the only cookware made from Pyroceram the, 'space-age ceramic – heat proof, cold proof and completely non-porous'. 'Housewives can reduce their cooking temperatures by 25 degrees Fahrenheit and still get the same results,' said Jobling's. What's more, one lock-on handle fitted the range of pan sizes. Thirty years on, this almost complete set with its original cookery book is a collector's gem. **£30-50**

WASHING POWDER

Self-service shopping, which took off in this decade, meant it was up to you to choose the groceries for your basket. This meant that rival firms had to make sure their products caught your eye. Daz soap powder first appeared in 1953, but this sixties packet shows how it wasn't just a case of bright branding. A decade later, you had to have exclusive extras too. In this case product manufacturers, Lever Brothers offered a tempting ½lb free! **£12 (unopened)**

Run your fingers over the raised blue and indented white stripes on this covered butter dish and you've got a big clue to its maker – the Derbyshire pottery, T.G. Green Ltd (founded 1864). Although Cornish Ware is believed to date from 1926, this dish falls into the firm's 1967 redesign (part of an attempt to boost flagging sales). Judith Onions, a young Royal College of Art graduate, was given the task of restyling Cornish Ware to make it more appealing for sixties homes. She came up with distinctive geometric shapes, angled knobs and curved handles, and a new factory mark (the 'target', with three bold concentric circles in the middle) was added to signify the move forward. Only a few years ago Cornish Ware popped up at car boot sales for pennies. But nostalgic collectors, keen to rekindle memories of their mother's kitchen, have pushed prices up to well over £600 for rarities. Traditional shapes in the new-wave fifties colours ('sunlit yellow', red, black, gold and green) carry a premium because they weren't as common as blue and white. It won't be too long before Onions' 1967 redesign shoots up in price too. Chips reduce an item's value considerably and do check the marks; T.G. Green had many imitators. **£20-30**

Visitors to the popular *Daily Mail* Ideal Home Exhibition in 1961 were the first to see British firm Creda's revolutionary new 'Constellation' cooker priced at 105 guineas (close to £5,000 today). With two ovens side by side it was a modern range-style cooker with the very latest accessories. The best feature was its 'Rosta-Spit', which was handy for barbecues and simply clipped onto the meat pan. Creda (est. 1898) claimed this innovative extra was, 'The most nearly perfect method of retaining the full flavoursome juices in food.' This oven is in good original condition, there are no chips on the enamel and it still works. It's a rarely seen must-have for a true sixties devotee. **£60-80**

SUNBEAM MULTI COOKER

Originally on sale for £13 2s 7d, this automatic Multi Cooker from Sunbeam was far cheaper than a conventional oven and ideally suited for modern 'fast and portable' cooking. In a limited space it could happily fry, stew, bake, boil, roast, braise, steam and even prepare a complete meal for six people promising 'no burnt offerings'. The only task it couldn't manage was the washing up afterwards! As *House Beautiful* magazine pointed out at the time, it was 'not, perhaps, suitable for cooking in front of your husband's boss but it's fun and fast for less starchy entertaining'. The American market was treated to these way before us and their versions even appeared with pastel-coloured handles. Possessing the original brochure is a bonus. **£10-12**

BRAUN JUICER

The Braun Multipress juicer is already an accepted design classic. Styled by Gerd Alfred Muller (1932-91), it not only looked good but was easy to use too. This sixties model (MP32) shows off Muller's very practical design. Knowing those who owned one would give it regular use, he made sure there were no tiny spaces for the odd bit of juicy orange flesh to linger. Before you'd even thought about making a mess, the splash guard around the central juice extractor stepped in and deflected the juice to collect in exactly the right place. Of course, an early model like this was an expensive luxury for the average home (£15 11s 6d) so there are relatively few survivors. **£100-120**

Marguerite Patten Presents a compact, colourful guide to home cooking — a treasury of favourite recipes to delight your family all the year round

THE FAMILY COOKBOOK

Marguerite Patten was the doyenne of home cooking in the fifties and sixties. Her regular appearances on BBC Radio's *Woman's Hour* and her own afternoon BBC TV show, *Cookery Club*, made her a household name and 'kitchen agony aunt'. *The Family Cookbook* (1964) is just one of her many publications now sought after by kitchenware collectors as a symbol of the period. **£4**

in the kitchen

THE MAGIMIX

The Magimix made by the French firm Robot Coupe (est. 1960), seems such a part of our lives today that it's hard to believe it first appeared over twenty years ago. When it was launched in Britain in 1974, many said it was ugly and would never last. But this clever machine achieved such notoriety in the professional catering field that it was sure to be a success at home. Within two years the Magimix had become a cult item despite its £79 price tag, which put it way beyond the cost of the average mixer. It was branded a 'cuisine systeme' (kitchen system) with blades, slicers, graters and whisks all revolving in the base of one bowl. The powerful 800-watt induction motor, tough plastic bowl (made from the same polycarbonate plastic as Concorde's windows) and the stainless steel Sabatier knife promised to last a lifetime. Robot Coupe recognized that cooking and presentation were now considered more important than laborious preparation. For collectors, only pristine examples of the first run of models like this will stand the test of time. **£30-40**

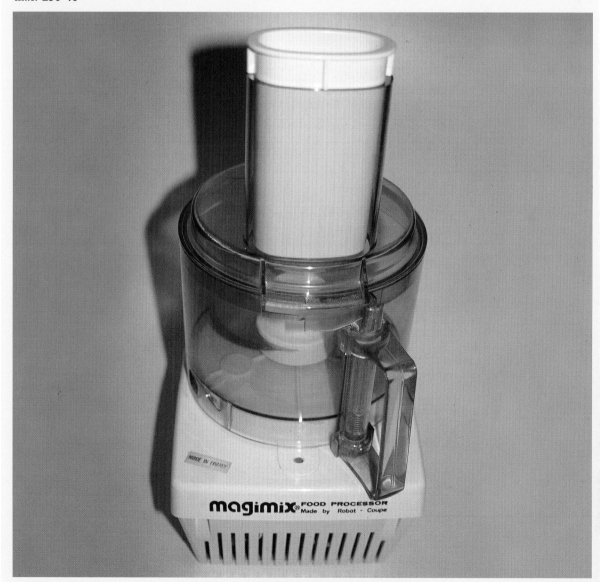

Textiles played an important part in seventies interior design and the fabric-look even extended to trays. The appropriately named 'Fab' tray on the right is made from 'a carefully chosen decorator's fabric' sealed in plastic. Look for original labels to identify the maker – in this case the one on the left is a Hardy Glenwood Production from Canada. **£5**

English fashion designer Barbara Hulaniki (b.1936) attracted a lot of attention when she opened her flagship Biba store in London's trendy High Street Kensington. As well as a retail outlet for her famous 'Biba' label clothes, this high street store, spread over six floors, had a restaurant, food store and children's ware departments. Here you could purchase anything from a tin of Biba paint and a roll of wallpaper to a take-home meal. This brown carrier bag is an unusual and rare surviving reminder of the Biba store's heyday before it shut down in 1975. Promoting the famous below stairs food hall it's a piece that completes the Biba picture for a growing band of collectors. This Biba matchbox still contains its original matches. **£10 (paper bag) £3 (matchbox)**

Fred the Homepride Man was a clever creation designed to put Homepride flour at the forefront of every housewife's mind. Buy a bag of flour and you had an offer that was difficult to refuse (from 1969): for six tokens and a mere 3/6 (around 17p today) you could have a Fred plastic flour shaker like this one made by the British toymakers Airfix (est. 1939). Five hundred thousand took up the offer, which was followed by a salt and pepper set and hundreds of other Fred mementoes made by numerous firms throughout the seventies. Today they are being snapped up by a growing number of Fred devotees. Check for the Airfix mark on the bottom, which signifies an early Fred, and also make sure the arms and hands are secure – they had a nasty habit of dropping off. **£12-15 each**

21

The blue and yellow floral decoration on this English Taunton Vale storage jar reflects the seventies mood. From vinyl wallpaper to humble containers like this one, introducing patterns was a way of transforming your kitchen. They were usually based on Art Nouveau styles or were an interpretation of the exotic patterns that came out of India and the Third World. Keen collectors are quietly stockpiling Taunton Vale for the future. So complete sets in graduating sizes are becoming harder to find. **£4-8 each**

Italian designer Marco Zanuso (b.1916) proved how even the most humdrum piece of kitchen equipment (in this case, kitchen scales) could be transformed with the right styling. No more lurking in the corner for these. With vivid orange ABS plastic for the body of his 4000 series scales, they could hardly stand out more. They were made around 1973 by the French firm Terraillon and incorporated another clever touch. The lid also doubled as the measuring pan. Look out for other colours including yellow too. **£40-50**

Country browns for a rural-style seventies kitchen were what designer John Clappison's 'Saffron' pattern for Britain's Hornsea Pottery was all about. He used a 'resist' technique so that the glaze wouldn't stick properly to the screen-printed decoration, creating the raised effect you see here. This tea, coffee and sugar storage trio dates from 1974 (although 'Saffron' first appeared in 1970). It lasted well into the eighties, but by that stage it was considered dated. Now Hornsea is experiencing a revival and attracting collectors' eyes, so keep yours peeled for it. **£12-15 (trio)**

PYREX TUMBLERS

Perfect for hot or cold drinks, plastic-cased 'Drink-Ups' were relative newcomers to Pyrex's 'oven to table' glassware range. They came in fashionable colours and stood out from cheap imported imitations because they offered a two-year guarantee.

The seventies was a key decade for British Pyrex after the American Corning Corporation (where Pyrex began) bought James A. Jobling and changed the firm's name to Corning Ltd. As a result the Jobling mark was dropped after 1975; giving you a clue to dating. **£5 (boxed)**

YOGHURT MAKER

A movement for healthy eating and self-sufficiency gathered widespread support in the seventies. Spurred on by the BBC's popular comedy series *The Good Life,* which began in 1975, Tom and Barbara wannabes stopped buying and started making. This electric Salton yoghurt maker cost £9 new. With its glass pots (rather than plastic) it was considered one of the finer models and produced supermarket-quality yoghurt for a fraction of the price. *Which?* magazine reported it cost around ½p to make one natural, 'health-giving' batch; a vast saving on the fourteen pence charged by the shops for a single carton. **£10+**

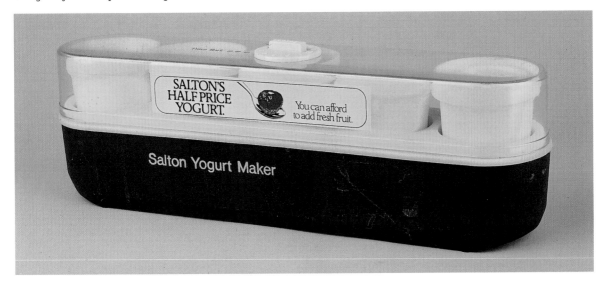

Modern material used in a modern way is the essence of the Egg-O-Tic egg cup-cum-salt-cellar (neatly tucked away in the lid). Moulded in polypropylene, it was designed by Maya Kissoczy and Carsten Joergensen for the Swiss firm Bodum in 1985. With a history that dates back to 1944, Bodum is known for products which offer great design at affordable prices and all are obvious collectables. **£2.25**

Furio Minuti designed this supremely stylish cutlery holder for the Italian firm, Guzzini. Founded in 1912, Guzzini made their first kitchen utensils from ox horn before progressing to using hot-moulded and then

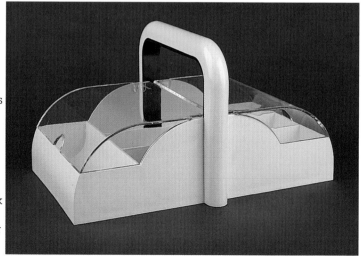

injection-moulded plastics. This holder is the centrepiece of their popular Papillon range, which was first seen in our stores in 1988. Its sleek look and clean white body fitted with modern living. And its resilient but elegant plastic base meant it was perfect for informal party use, indoors or out. The range, which came in other colours too, also included napkin holders, vacuum jugs, a paper-plate holder, and a holder for paper cups. Today Papillon pieces are desirable for their design and since discontinuation in 1993 are on the list of plastic collectables. Beware of cracks and scratches, look out for the 'Guzzini' Gs mark (four 'G's' linked together), and try to find pieces, like this one, which come with their original box. **£10-15**

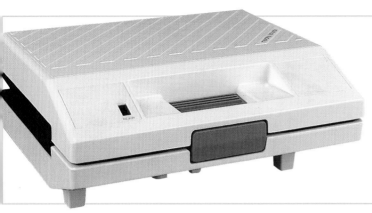

Handy hot snacks fresh from a sandwich toaster like this were all the rage. It took just two minutes to make something that tasted delicious with crisp toasted bread on the outside sealing in the hot filling inside. Daily use has meant a battering for most but this one by Morphy Richards has survived unscratched with its original box too! **£5**

The eighties fad for healthy eating meant special diets. And what could be better for a slimmer than Avery's electronic kitchen health scale? In 1984 it brought sophisticated microchip technology into the home and with the press of a button displayed the calorie, carbohydrate, fat and fibre content of over a thousand foods. But at £49.95 it was an expensive luxury and few survive today. Check that any examples you do see come with their instruction manual, which contained the code tables essential for operating the diet computer – otherwise you're stuck! **£15 (if complete)**

ALESSI WHISTLING KETTLE

When Italian Giovanni Alessi founded the company that bears his name in 1921 little did he know how sought after his designs would become. Taking risks where others won't, Alessi has succeeded in mass producing a vast range of items to meet our everyday needs in a strikingly different way. This 'Whistling' kettle by German designer Richard Sapper (b.1932) is held in high esteem by modern design gurus, particularly as Sapper spent three years perfecting its unique singing whistle! The 'Whistling' kettle has already gone down in history as a cult object of the eighties (and they're still sold now). Tempting though it is to use these, the advice is don't because in the future they'll be judged by their condition and that of their packaging.
£100 (200cl) £125 (300cl)

TEFAL'S LE SAUCIER

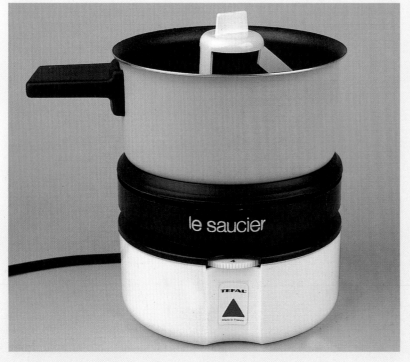

For inexperienced cooks with no time to spare, Tefal's (est. 1953) Le Saucier was invaluable. Suitable for any novice, all you had to do was pop the basic ingredients in the sauce pot and walk away. Like a slow cooker, Le Saucier gradually heated up and ensured the sauce stayed lump-free by stirring it constantly. The only thing you had to worry about was the cleaning afterwards – which was fairly cumbersome as the electrical appliance could not be immersed in water and the bowl was not removable! That may have contributed to its limited sales and discontinuation from Tefal's range a decade later. A true eighties piece of convenience equipment with styling to match, the Le Saucier (if you can find one) is already collected. **£7-10**

FREELINE KETTLE

With the arrival of the Yuppie (Young Urban [or Upwardly Mobile] Professional), technology suddenly needed to be as slick as its users. This Freeline kettle, launched in 1987 by Tefal (est. 1953), was the world's first cordless electric kettle. Its clean structured lines – a move away from the traditional jug shape – bear all the hallmarks of the great design team behind it, Richard Seymour and Dick Powell. In Powell's words 'this was a great idea because it solved a problem that we didn't realize we had'. Using the technology that already existed for cordless irons, the Seymour Powell partnership worked within strict safety standards to create a kettle that ingeniously cut the electric supply as soon as it was picked up. It may seem ordinary to us now (with over 60 per cent of all kettles sold being cordless) but, little more than a decade ago, this kettle was revolutionary. The original design, with a round knob on the lid rather than the later UK plug shape and the original three-light bars with an LED underneath, is worth looking for. Even before the first year was up, cost savings in design saw these features modified. **£15**

RUSSELL HOBBS

This milk warmer and coffee percolator, both by Russell Hobbs (their model CP2), was a development of the first automatic electric percolator. Boiling water is forced up through the coffee grounds. The brewed coffee then drips back down and is boiled again. To enliven the design of their percolator Russell Hobbs linked up with the famous Wedgwood pottery in Stoke-on-Trent to give it a modern look. In the late 1960s the coffee pot and matching milk warmer came in two patterns (Avon and Sierra) but this set dates from around 1983. The fact that it wasn't a best seller adds to its collectability. **£15-20 (for the pair)**

DYSON VACUUM CLEANER

Dyson's famous bagless vacuum cleaner may have only been around since 1993 but it's made such an impression in our homes already that it won't be long before we're talking about doing the 'dysoning' rather than the 'hoovering'! Sheer technical innovation (it was the first of its kind) plus good design has seen James Dyson's DC02 (Dual Cyclone cylinder model) become Britain's top-selling vacuum cleaner. It took 5,127 prototypes to reach launch stage but once there, the public and museums snapped it up. 'I developed great admiration for engineers like Buckminster Fuller and Isambard Kingdom Brunel. They made me realize that it was not enough to be just a designer, you had to be an engineer as well,' says Dyson. You also need to be clever. Limited runs of premium priced, special versions like this De Stijl DC02 (launched 1996 and named after the Dutch avant-garde art group) have helped to maintain a contemporary feel. They're also the ones to go for because far fewer of these are made when compared with the standard grey and yellow model. **£249.99**

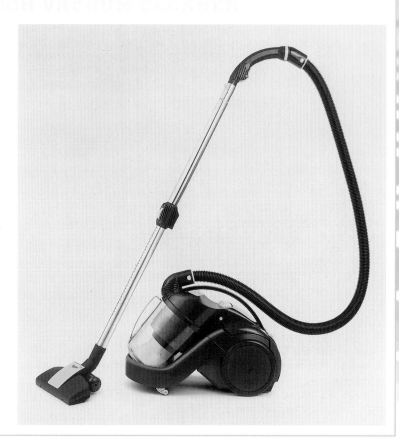

ENVIRONMENT-FRIENDLY PACKAGING

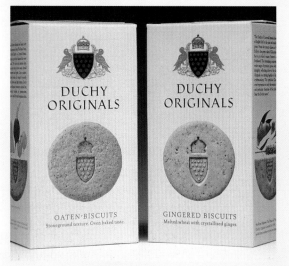

Concerns about the environment and the quality of our food have been mirrored by a corresponding surge of interest in organic products. Ten years ago they were confined to specialist health food stores. Now organic products are supermarket sellers with expanding mass-market appeal. The packaging of these Oaten Biscuits made by Duchy Originals Limited (to benefit the Prince of Wales's Charitable Foundation) embodies the contemporary mood. The environment-friendly packaging is made from recycled paper and the biscuits themselves are 'super green', using organic wheat and oats grown on His Royal Highness's farm at Highgrove. In the same way we cherish pre-war biscuit tins, fifty years from now it could be these. Most of us munch the contents then recycle the packaging but some clever people have already kept those first packets from their launch in 1992 (recognizable because the printed contents weight is 300g rather than the 250g now). **£1.95**

The last years of the nineteenth century attracted all sorts of commemoratives to mark the dawn of a new age and the millennium promises to do just the same, albeit on a far grander scale. Russell Hobbs' sleek new 'Millennium' kettle, which appeared in September 1996, is one we're bound to remember. In the same way that advanced fifties products were fashionably branded 'Constellation', 'Orbit' or featured Space Age motifs, 'millennium' is swiftly becoming the buzz word for the very latest nineties gadgets. Described as 'the kettle of the future – available now', it uses revolutionary new technology to make it the fastest boiler around. Instead of the conventional element there's a steel disc with tiny imprinted tracks to directly heat the water. Add this kettle to a range of other millennium commemoratives and you'll have a fascinating collection for the future. **£36.99 (original classic white) £39.99 (for the later blue, green, yellow and peppermint versions)**

Nostalgia for sixties inflatables no doubt encouraged Michael Sodeau from British design team Inflate to come up with this blow-up PVC egg cup. At its launch in 1995 it was an instant hit, sealing the success of their novel range of household blow-ups. Inflate's aim, as you can see here, is to come up with objects that are 'original, fun, functional and affordable' and enhance the quality of our life. Mass market these may be, but they are also fragile. Take the head off your egg too fast with a sharp knife and it could be a disaster! Years from now how many will have survived intact? **£10 (for four)**

With a catalogue of household goodies that comes close to matching the thickness of a telephone directory, Italian design giant Alessi has gone from strength to strength this decade. Astute collectors are already squirreling away as much as they can because the Alessi look is so new, so distinctive and so well made. It's also so nineties with its bright colours, polished steel, pressure cast aluminium and thermoplastic. Key names such as Italian designer Alessandro Mendini (b.1931) are brought in to give mass-produced products like the 'Anna Pepper' mill (1998) a personality that begs to be bought. Like Dinky toys, they come in all colour variations to satisfy collectors; the only limiting factor is how many you can afford (they are quality designer items and are priced as such). **£37**

Branded 'serious tools for funny people' the Zoo range of kitchen utensils cleverly combines quality materials (expensive ABS plastic and stainless steel) with ergonomic design and a touch of whimsical styling. They're pure nineties treasures whose vibrant colours signal a move away from the black and chromes that dominated kitchens a decade ago. Who else but the great American gadget makers Ekco (est. 1888) and their designers from the celebrated Ancona 2, Inc could come up with a jar-opener shaped like a shark and a spoon that looks like a giraffe? Kitchenware collectors prize turn-of-the-century enamelled utensils (dull by comparison) sold for pennies then but now worth around £30 a piece. Add to that the surge of interest in plastic design and you're looking at a range of grown-up toys that deserve to be kept.
£2.95-8.95 each (there are twenty-six in all)

Retro fifties colours are given a nineties twist with modern plastics by Italian firm Guzzini (founded 1912) in their inspired 'Gildo' mini-chopper. It first appeared along with its cousins (a hand blender, toaster and tabletop grill) in 1997, the brainchild of Italian designer D. Tanfoglio. Success has seen another five pieces join the undeniably stylish 'Gildo' family (a juicer, Parmesan grater, crumb vacuum, contact grill and hand mixer). Each is available in mix and match pastels (yellow, green and more recently blue). But the white version is the one to hold on to – it's set to be discontinued.
£59.95

Any day soon we'll see another revolution in vacuum cleaners when the Swedish company Electrolux take us into the twenty-first century with the world's first robotic vacuum cleaner tailor-made for the home. Set to become a standard item, it automatically bags dirt using its brain (a microprocessor) to navigate around your furniture. It may be futuristic but users already say, 'It's brilliant because I can take my boys to school and go to work, and I know when I get back, my carpet will be clean.' Be there when the first models are launched late in 1999. This prototype is one of only two made and is set to become a museum piece. It's early days for prices but Electrolux are the world's largest manufacturer of vacuums so it's sure to be affordable.
In the region of £500

After three hit films, *A Grand Day Out* (1989), *The Wrong Trousers* (1993) and *A Close Shave* (1995), plus a string of awards including three Oscars for creator Nick Park, popular Plasticine duo Wallace and Gromit are international stars. The merchandising they've spawned is one of the nineties hottest collectables because much of it, such as these fridge magnets, is sold in limited edition runs. Made by Giftware International (under licence from Aardman Animations and the BBC) this set was priced at £14.99 when it was sold exclusively for a brief period (July-December 1994) in Boots stores. Subsequent alterations to the packaging means this red box is talked about in collectors' circles. Proof that you don't have to spend a fortune to find worthwhile material. **£20+**

An unforgettable read from an unforgettable British chef that's as absorbing as his food. *White Heat* (1993) was the first book by Marco Pierre White (b.1962) and it marked a major new direction in food writing. He shot to fame as the world's newest and most exciting chef, and in 1990, aged just twenty-seven, he became the youngest chef ever to be awarded two Michelin stars. *White Heat's* dramatic full-page photographs by Bob Carlos Clarke (b. 1950) are an invitation to drool. The text is bittersweet, mixing White's straight talking with his sumptuous collection of recipes – from a sexy behind-the-scenes viewpoint. Hard-backed first editions like the copy on the left (published by Pyramid Books) are already like gold dust as they're only available in paperback now. **£25+ (hardback)**

IN THE

Dining Room

In the post-war home, when dinner parties with the boss smoothed career paths for countless husbands, the dining room was a key player. For the house-proud hostess it was the room where she could show off her culinary skills to perfection, in the shape of richly sauced delights with a refreshing Continental touch, served on the finest china. It was vital that the overall effect was dazzlingly modern. In the fifties that meant having the very latest tableware and cutlery, being a 'natural' at arranging a floral centrepiece, and splashing out on a new dress for the occasion.

By the time the decade was in full swing, Utility restrictions on fancy wares for the domestic market had been lifted. In the high street, stores like Boots the Chemist, then a major force in homewares, and Woolworth's tempted housewives back with modern tableware that wouldn't break the bank. American and Scandinavian style was a must, and galactic motifs, organic asymmetrical outlines and brightly coloured patterns were guaranteed to gain admiration from your guests.

British pottery giant, Midwinter, epitomized the new taste in dining with their distinctly different 'Stylecraft' china. Out went the traditional round plate and in came modernism in the form of a practical, stackable, TV-shaped alternative. Starter sets suited newly-weds on a budget, whilst there were break-resistant versions in Melamine for those who valued durability. It was a mix 'n' match affair right down to the furniture. With the new G-Plan range, homeowners could choose precisely which dining accessories they wanted rather than accepting a standard showroom suite.

By the sixties dining had adopted a new direction. Instead of being linked to the kitchen by a serving hatch, the dining room became an extension of the cooking space via a walk-through arch. Modern French-style casseroles sparked an array of resilient geometrically-shaped oven-to-tableware dishes that matched the household china.

Whether it was a lamp, vase or coffee pot, there was one shape that counted in the sixties – the cylinder. Even teapots and teacups took on the new cylindrical line that was perfect for decoration – white space was covered with anything from lava-lamp blobs of colour and psychedelic patterns to ethnic florals.

'Bon viveur' entertaining was even more fashionable if you owned something made from stainless steel – providing it was cylindrical of course! As the seventies arrived the British Steel Corporation took part in the *Daily Mail* Ideal Home Exhibition for the first time. Their 'Steel in the Home' stand, styled by the Conran Design Group, introduced the public to this 'sophisticated and versatile material'.

Gone were the days when solid silver and plated cutlery was in vogue. By the seventies the booming number of households that owned dishwashers demanded easy-clean stainless steel on their tables. Tableware reflected this more relaxed attitude to eating by becoming truly multi-purpose. A Denby soup bowl, for instance, worked perfectly as a dessert dish too, and a vegetable tureen neatly doubled as a bread and butter pudding server. Pottery as a whole had a solid, earthy feel about it, which fitted well with the wave of enthusiasm for self-sufficiency and vegetarianism.

In the fast-moving eighties where time was of the essence for growing numbers of career women, microwave dishes were a godsend. Even the smartest tableware was graced with perfectly steamed vegetables cooked the electronic way. Against a backdrop of predominantly white china and simple dining furniture, eating was a colourful feast, although fashionable nouvelle cuisine portions were minute. The idea of display was conveyed through 'designer' dining accessories. Alessi tableware styled by key architects and Italian 'Memphis Group' dining tables to match kept the young professionals and their guests happy.

With an eye on the future, the nineties dining room was geared to adaptability. Nigel Coates's 'Oyster House' unveiled at the 1998 Ideal Home Exhibition introduced the concept of an open-plan environment where dinner-party style entertaining still had a part to play. Once the guests had left, his slim-line 'Oyster' dining chairs and table could be repositioned in another room, for instance, to suit family life.

Hence, the static dining room of the fifties gave way to a multi-purpose space, four decades on. Recycled tableware (widely available from leading interiors stores like Habitat and Heals) has a part to play, whilst glass and perspex are at the cutting edge of dining fashion in the drive for a less cluttered look. Every good nineties hostess relies on quality accessories – like the varied Conran Collection – to impress.

DENBY POTTERY

One of the most striking studio ranges to come out of Britain's famous Denby pottery (founded 1809) this decade was 'Cheviot', the work of in-house designer Glyn Colledge (b.1922). A Perrier bottle was behind the look of these swan-necked vases that matched the range's bowls, trays and platters. The abstract sgraffito (or etched) pattern on a matt glaze echoes the fifties fascination for astronomy and space so clearly laid out in the Festival of Britain's 'Outer Space' exhibition. Cheviot appeared shortly before the BBC broadcast its first *Sky at Night* programme and the Space Age officially began with Russia's launch of Sputnik-1 (the world's first artificial satellite), both in 1957 and, with it, Colledge captured the contemporary mood. Look carefully at the decoration and you'll spot stars mixed in with more earthly leaf designs. These vases may have cost £4.10s then but, spurred on by museum interest, they can be worth a hundred times that now! Rather than the standard Denby mark on the base, look for Glyn Colledge's script signature in blue. **£80 (bowl) £100-400 (vase)**

SUSIE COOPER

British ceramics designer Susie Cooper (1902-95) was equally star-struck and her popular etched 'Scrolls' pattern from 1955, decorating this bone china cruet set, was clearly inspired by astronomy. She even added a star to one of the pottery's back–stamps.
£40-60 (cruet set)

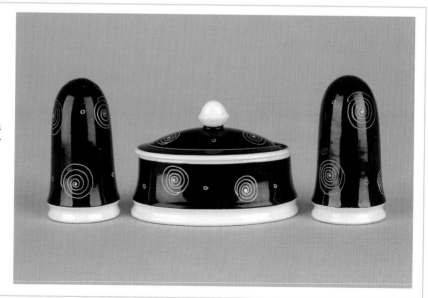

'HOMEMAKER'

With an upbeat name like 'Homemaker' (evoking much-admired American homestyle) the British Ridgway pottery (est. 1792) was looking for a hit. They got it when this tableware first appeared on the shelves of sole retailers, Woolworth's, in 1957. Enid Seeney's distinctive printed design, scattered with recognisable symbols of contemporary furniture – from Robin Day's Reclining Chair for Hille – to spindly legged plant stands, was refreshingly modern and temptingly cheap. Not surprisingly it found instant appeal amongst newlyweds who could afford to build up a stylish dinner service piece by piece. Because it was still made well into the late sixties, plenty survives today but much of it is knife scratched or chipped from use. Plates are fairly common while coffee pots are not so easy to find.

£12 (plate) £70 (coffee pot)

MELAMINE

As the 'Aesthetic of Plastics' stand at the 34th Milan Trade Fair (1956) and the British Plastics Exhibition (1957) proudly showed, the plastics industry was booming on a world-wide scale. At home, the gossip was all about melamine – that unbreakable and colourful plastic developed in the 1930s but not truly exploited on the domestic front until now. The plus points were that it could be moulded into anything from teacups to butter dishes and it was clearly more durable than most ceramics. But melamine was still expensive and needed serious advertising in Britain to overcome the price hurdle. Sceptics were swayed by claims that it could withstand rough daily use as shown by champion yachtsmen who 'chose' melamine for their notoriously tough sailing adventures. The fact that they were given pieces to wave-test by the manufacturers was glossed over! Today it's adored for its period look and pristine pieces with the 'Gaydon' (like this butter dish, made from a similar plastic called melmex), 'Melaware' and 'Argosy Ware' trademarks are snapped up. **£8-10**

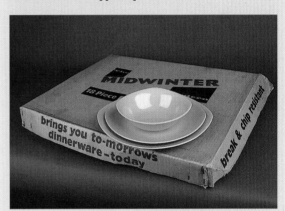

MIDWINTER'S 'STYLECRAFT'

Wartime utility restrictions were just being lifted when Midwinter's (est. 1910) revolutionary 'Stylecraft' tableware first caught the public's eye in 1953. Dining rooms could never be dull or chintzy again with the combination of Roy Midwinter's practical, stackable TV-shaped plate and the host of organic abstract patterns that decorated it. The result, as period adverts proudly said, was 'in perfect harmony with home décor'. The new 'fashion' shape (with rimless plates) appeared a year later. And Midwinter made use of both in-house designer Jessie Tait and freelance designers like Terence Conran (b.1931) (then a young graduate), Hugh Casson (b.1910) (architect and watercolourist) and Peter Scott (1902-89) (the bird painter) to style their range of modern patterns. Tait's polka-dot 'Red Domino' (right) is probably the best-known design but it's Tait's 'Primavera' and 'Festival' and Conran's 'Nature Study', 'Saladware' and 'Plant Life' patterns that fetch the top prices. Do watch out for look-a-like Stylecraft (similar patterns from other potteries). Check the base to make sure you've got an original 'Stylecraft' and not some poor relation! **£15-50 (dinner plate–depending on pattern) £12 (mug)**

'GREENWHEAT' POTTERY

'Greenwheat' was the Denby pottery's answer to the New Look. And the public couldn't seem to get enough of this hand-painted dinnerware that first appeared in 1956. Its hallmark, a spray of wheat-ears and leaves, was quite different from anything else on the market and it proved to be one of the firm's best-selling lines for over twenty years. Because so much was made for such a long time, it's the pieces that didn't sell well or were later modified that are prized today. The original gravy boat, for instance, was far too long and thin and it soon disappeared in favour of a round one.

£12 (dinner plate) £15+ (gravy boat) £9 (cup and saucer) £6 (egg cup) £25-30 (casserole)

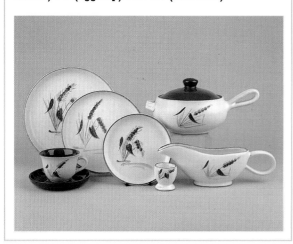

'PRIDE' CUTLERY SET

Cutlery sold in single settings as well as more expensive canteens made modern dining adaptable and affordable. In the case of British silversmith, David Mellor's (b.1930) now-famous 'Pride' range, cutlery sets came with bone or white xylonite handles meaning you could create a mix and match look. 'Pride' was developed while Mellor was still a student at London's Royal College of Art and got its first public airing at his final year degree show in 1954. With it, Mellor hoped to achieve a 'demonstrably modern design for silver cutlery' that was also ideal for mass-production. Sheffield-based Walker & Hall (where Mellor later became Design Director) saw Pride's potential even before the degree show was out. Their Chairman, Peter Inchbald, quickly gave the range a name – 'Pride' – and the firm started work on its manufacture. For collectors it helps that this set is still in its 'as new' condition with the original box. The fact that 'Pride' won a Council of Industrial Design, Design of the Year award in 1957 makes it even more desirable. About 98% of the Pride sets were silver-plated like this one to reach a broader market but the odd few were made to special order in silver and they'd be worth considerably more.

£225 (boxed silver-plated set)

ARNE JACOBSEN

It must have been a real relief to throw out that heavy pre-war furniture and replace it with a dining set like this by Danish designer Arne Jacobsen (1902-71). As light as a feather, the rosewood veneer dining chairs were from his famous 'Ant' series (1952), which used a single piece of steamed plywood to form the back and the seat. No joints or stretchers meant it was easy to mass-produce. Early versions like these followed the contemporary asymmetrical look with their three legs. They're marked 'F.H. Danmark' (for the chairs) and 'Made in Denmark by F.H.' plus a Danish flag transfer (for the table) to acknowledge their manufacturer, Fritz Hansen. Don't mix them up with today's ant chair reproductions (with four legs) sold in a spectrum of vivid colours.

£800 (table and chairs)

G-PLAN

G-plan was synonymous with 'flexible furnishing' for the home. Why buy a matching suite of furniture when you could choose individual pieces (all G-plan of course) that were tailor-made to go together? So, for instance, you could match this G-plan dining table (with space-saving flaps) and chairs with your choice of sideboard. Not surprisingly the modular idea quickly caught on and E. Gomme Ltd, the Buckinghamshire furniture makers, did a roaring trade throughout the decade. G-plan was by no means top of the range designer quality, but it was mid-market expensive and warded off cheap imitations with the official G-plan stamp. It's early days for collecting G-plan, but don't wait too long as interest is increasing.

£50-80

CARLTON WARE'S ORBIT

'Orbit' was one of Carlton Ware's (est. 1890 as Wiltshaw & Robinson) most successful new-look fifties lines. The plates, cups and coffee pot all have a distinctive triangular shape with cherry red coloured glaze and space-inspired pattern designed by Peter Forster. It may be attractive but compared to pre-war Carlton Ware, which can sell for thousands, this range is cheap collect it now while you can!

£25-30 (jam pot)
£30-50 (sugar sifter)
£30-40 (salt and pepper)
£45-60 (coffee pot)
£15-20 (cup and saucer)

TAPIO WIRKKALA

Only a very small number of these laminated birch platters were made by Finnish designer Tapio Wirkkala (b.1915) in 1954. And demand must have outstripped supply by a long way after one of his early creations was voted 'Most Beautiful Object of the Year' 1951 by interiors magazine *House Beautiful*. Today, nothing's changed, few have survived and collectors prize those that have. **£2,000**

HORNSEA POTTERY

This large 'White Bud' vase from Hornsea Pottery's 'Home Décor' range was one of the most stylish flower holders around. Although John Clappison (b.1937) came up with its very distinctive raised dot design and splayed symmetrical outline in 1958, it remained on the firm's lists until 1962 – the textured decoration fitted well with sixties homes too. Don't worry if there are dots of brown staining inside – that's where the metal cage to support the flower stems attached – all part of its provenance or history. **£300**

POOLE POTTERY

Poole pottery's (est. 1895) fluid Freeform range launched in 1956 was aimed directly at those who fancied a very modern floral touch on the table. Flower arranging was the latest craze – you could learn about it at Constance Spry's flower school, and see it in practice at Heal's exhibitions. And these vases were perfect, so the adverts said, for the 'graceful arrangement of foliage or blossoms'. Alfred Burgess Read (1898-1973) and Guy Sydenham came up with the abstract Freeform shapes to rival Scandinavia's modern ceramics, which were proving so popular. With new contemporary patterns to match, like 'Bamboo' designed by Alfred's daughter, Ann, and 'Totem' by Ruth Pavely, Poole was catapulted into the international arena. Fortunately for us, Poole was so proud of its handiwork that genuine pieces carry the firm's backstamp and usually the painters' marks too – in this case the decoration on both vases was Gwen Haskins' handiwork. **£350-500 ('Bamboo' vase) £700-900 ('Totem' vase)**

SIDEBOARD

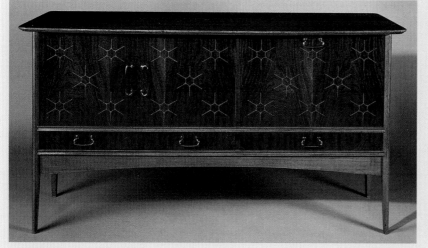

A dining room was incomplete without a sideboard. And this low-slung one by British designer Peter Hayward for W.G.Evans & Sons (founded 1936) attracted serious attention when it was shown at the Ideal Home Exhibition in 1956. Elegant tapering legs (almost 18th century in feel) were a signature of the decade as was the rosewood veneer on the front. Here it's cut away with a router to reveal fashionable star motifs in lighter birchwood beneath. **£2,250**

the Sixties

DENBY'S ARABESQUE

Pastels and 'gay' primary colours may well have ruled fifties style but a decade later it was earthy browns, olive greens and moody blues that counted. Few ceramics evoke the true feel of this era more than Denby pottery's 'Arabesque' oven to tableware, dreamed up by their resident designer Gill Pemberton (b.1936) after her trip to Russia in 1962. Denby aimed high with this rich almost bejewelled design, promoting it ostentatiously as a must-have luxury. Those young marrieds who were given Arabesque first time round are probably still using it. But now it's attracting a second generation of would-be collectors. What a change from a few years ago when unwanted Arabesque wasn't even worthy of jumble! **£11 (dinner plate) £15-40 (coffee pot) £55+ (ice bucket – very rare) up to £55 (14" chop platter) £5 (mugs) £6.50 (creamer) £5-15 (accessory pieces)**

MIDWINTER'S 'SPANISH GARDEN' TABLEWARE

Midwinter's best selling 'Spanish Garden' tableware shows how it wasn't just the colours of the fifties that were now dated, but the shapes had moved on apace too. Cylindrical forms with straight sides and flat lids were ideal for vast amounts of transfer-printed decoration – a key element of the 'Swinging Sixties' look. David Queensbury (b.1929) and Roy Midwinter (1923-90) were behind this 'Fine' shape, which appeared in 1962. The most memorable pattern to decorate it, which was almost psychedelic in look, was 'Spanish Garden' (available from 1966). The public couldn't get enough of it on china, cake tins and even saucepans. Most likely they were spurred on by seeing it used in the popular BBC comedy series *Sykes* a few years later. Surprisingly the rarest pieces for collectors are mugs, because they were the first things to get broken. **£7 (dinner plate) £20 (tureen) £7 (mug)**

TEAK

Just as the fifties were devoted to Formica, dark woods dominated the sixties. Teak salad bowls like this one, carved with wood fresh from Bangkok were a good match for top-selling walnut and rosewood veneered furniture. Period style magazines showed how these pieces looked 'striking against light walls'. Because teak supplies were plentiful it appeared everywhere, even on the finial of this plastic lampshade (below) (there were only the faintest concerns about the effects tree-felling would ultimately have on the environment). Their value is relatively low because neither have marks and the bowl is rather crudely made but to a sixties collector they have potential. **£10 (bowl) £15 (lampshade)**

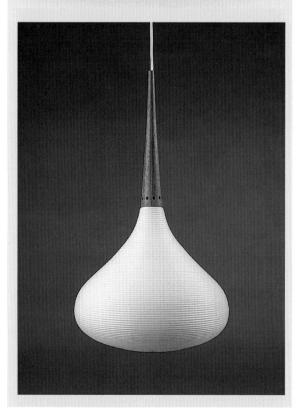

POOLE POTTERY'S 'DELPHIS BOWL'

This Poole pottery bowl was one of the firm's new studio pieces, which was sold as 'Delphis' after its launch at Heals in October 1963. The studio range which really captured sixties style, was the brainchild of resident designer, Frank Jefferson, senior thrower Guy Sydenham and later the designer and painter Tony Morris. To show how modern Poole could be they took the key shapes of the decade and transformed them into pottery. Tapering vases based on cylinders, circular bowls and the distinctive lozenge-shaped sweet dish were all hand-decorated with vivid abstract patterns and made either as one-off experimental pieces or limited studio editions. 'No two pieces are alike,' claimed one factory leaflet. It was the bright colours (that got even brighter and shinier as the decade progressed) that were such a feature of Delphis. However, early sixties glazes (the orange made from toxic uranium) were unstable and blistered on the surface, which provides a good guide to dating. Also look for the Poole factory mark (it may read 'studio') on the bottom – if the dolphin is blue it's likely to be early Delphis which is sought-after. Combined with the dolphin you may find the intertwined initials of the painter; key names worth having are Robert Jefferson (rj), Tony Morris (TM intertwined), Christian Tate (cT intertwined) and Carole Holden (C and CH).
£400-500 (14" bowl, unknown painter)

'SMOKE' GLASSES

For all those who couldn't manage without a cigarette while drinking, Italian designer Joe Colombo (1930-71) came up with these aptly named 'Smoke' glasses. The off-balance foot neatly fitted into the palm of your hand meaning you only needed to wrap your thumb round the stem to hold it in place. That left your other fingers free... for a cigarette, of course! Needless to say this inspired creation won seven design awards and has already made it into museum collections around the world. The fact that this set still has its manufacturer's and designer's labels plus its original box puts it a cut above the rest.
£700 (for the set of 12)

'CARNABY DAISY' AND 'HARLEQUINADE'

Great British potter Susie Cooper could never be accused of failing to keep up with the times. The 'Carnaby Daisy' pattern (1968) on these teacups and saucers (right) proved that even at the ripe old age of 66, she was still intune with the in-crowd. Together with Sir Paul Reilly from the Design Council, Susie ventured to London on a fact-finding mission. And Carnaby Daisy was the result, influenced by the vibrancy of the capital city's popular fashion venue, Carnaby Street. Another design that was shockingly modern was her psychedelic 'Harlequinade' pattern (below) with its overlapping lava-lamp-style blobs of colour (also 1968). By now Susie Cooper's own company had been absorbed by the ceramics giant, Wedgwood and the marks change to credit that connection. Both these patterns are rarely seen and are avidly sought-after now with the bulk of any pieces that do survive going straight to collectors in Japan.
£30 ('Carnaby Daisy' teacup and saucer)
£50 ('Harlequinade' teacup and saucer)

MOULDED PLASTIC

With dining furniture like this, German design team Farner and Grunder (for American furniture manufacturer Herman Miller) showed that moulded plastic could be transformed into something supremely elegant. The vivid orange upholstery of the seat follows the curves of a single piece of plastic, which, although it doesn't look it, makes these chairs amazingly comfortable. Although used on a daily basis this set has survived in remarkably clean condition. **£1,000 (table and chair set)**

BEATLEMANIA

Star-struck Beatles fans could hardly forget their number one pop band with breakfast bowls like these. As Beatlemania struck, after the Beatles first UK chart-topping single 'Please, Please Me' (1963), so did the merchandising. The 'Fab Four's' distinctive mop-headed portraits were emblazoned over a host of official and unofficial mementoes. Britain's Washington Pottery Ltd. (founded 1946) was behind this set of six bowls while the Rolex Paper Company Ltd produced these paper napkins, complete with John, Paul, George and Ringo's facsimile signatures. To be of serious value it's important that merchandising like this has survived in good condition. These napkins, for instance, were obviously too precious for one fan to even think of using because they're still complete with their original cellophane wrapper. **£300-400 (bowls)**
£20-30 (paper napkins)

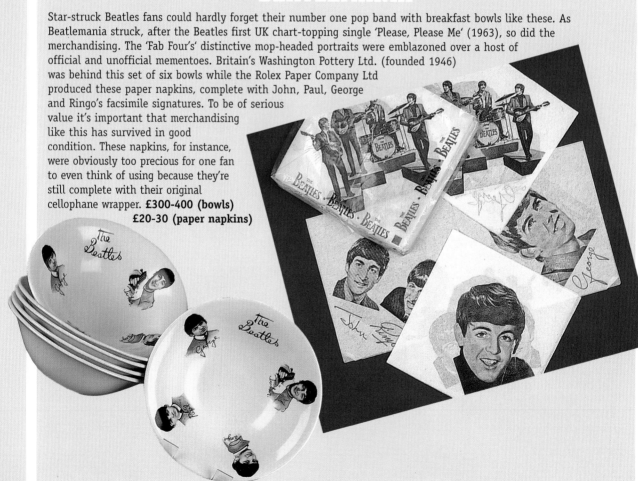

'OP ART' LAMP

The swirling pattern on this 'Flowerpot' lamp by Danish designer Verner Panton (b.1926) was definitely in tune with the psychedelic mood sweeping through Europe and America at the time. Made by Lüber in 1970 (after a version shown at the Louvre's 'What is Design?' exhibition in 1969) you can see how Panton was also interested in optical illusions and the Op Art movement that was popularised by British artist Bridget Riley (b. 1931). Stare hard enough, and the black and white swirls appear to be on different planes. **£300**

'CONCEPT' TABLEWARE

If you see a piece of Hornsea Pottery's distinctive 'Concept' tableware like this hang on to it, because Martin Hunt and Colin Rawson's inspired design was largely exported. The distinctive layered effect and swan-style knobs give it away. In 1977 the range was largely restricted to cream, but other colours soon followed, namely matt black ('Image'), grey and pink ('Swan Lake') and a pale blue design ('Cirrus'). Concept's sleek design helped to earn it a coveted Design Council Award in 1977, which is why it is collectable today. **£20 (cup and saucer) £50 (teapot)**

TUBULAR STEEL CHAIRS

Using cane for the back and seats of these tubular steel chairs (made in around 1979) conveyed a light, natural feel that fitted well with relaxed-looking interiors. German designer Stefan Wewkerka (b.1928) drew his inspiration from an accepted classic (in this case Marcel Breuer's B32 chair, a Bauhaus creation from 1928), but brought it up to date with a modern twist. Look carefully and you'll see that this seventies multi-purpose chair is asymmetrically styled for practicality. Collectors prefer complete dining sets and this chair is far more valuable accompanied by three chairs and a table. **£650 (matching set of four chairs and a table)**

'WILD OATS'

Easy, casual dining with an earthy feel was what Midwinter pottery's 'Stonehenge' shape was all about. When Roy Midwinter (1923-90) introduced settings like these in 1972 they were hailed as 'exciting' and 'daring'. The accompanying 'Wild Oats' pattern (above) was a perfect fit for the type of healthy living advocated by the BBC's popular comedy series *The Good Life* (1974-8). Tom and Barbara Good attempted their own version of self-sufficiency in the back garden of their home in the heart of suburban Surrey. For collectors it's patterns like 'Nasturtium' (below) that are worth seeking out. This was withdrawn from sale because the cadmium red glaze proved a health hazard for Midwinter's employees. The Midwinter mark on both patterns is impressed, so it's often difficult to see – you may have to look quite hard.
£10 ('Wild Oats' dinner plate) £30 (coffee pot) £15 ('Nasturtium' dinner plate)

'NASTURTIUM'

CUTLERY

With its patterned stoneware handles Denby's 'Touchstone' cutlery gave dining tables a co-ordinated look (when combined with matching Denby ceramics of course!). And the skill of the design team (Gill Pemberton and husband Neil Harding) was recognized when 'Touchstone' won a coveted Blue Ribbon Award for innovation at the *Daily Mail* Ideal Home Exhibition in 1976. A year later French designer, Jean-Pierre Vitrac (b.1944) threw conventional materials to the wind and came up with this disposable polystyrene eating set, intended for casual picnic meals. Each of the six brightly coloured individual place settings made up of a plate, three pieces of cutlery and a dessert pot moulded from a single plastic sheet – and they still remain attached in parts. Manufacturers Diam found out just how easy Vitrac's design was to mass-produce and they made these sets until 1980. But, as the disposable connection suggests, few have survived and a pristine, unbroken set like this is a rarity and already considered a museum piece. **£6+ a piece £35 (complete boxed set) £80-120 (plastic picnic set)**

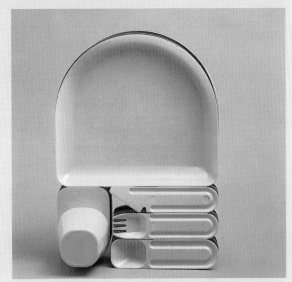

'BOCCIO' DINING SET

In 1973, the Arab OPEC nations (Organisation of Petroleum Exporting Countries) sent oil prices rocketing and sparked a global energy crisis. The effect on the plastics industry was dramatic and a material that a decade before had been so affordable it was actually disposable, suddenly became prohibitively expensive. That explains the rarity of this all-plastic 'Boccio' dining set. Italian manufacturer Ipi launched it just before the oil crisis in 1972. And although its organic lines probably made it the ultimate in dining comfort and its easy to stack, easy to interlock chairs were downright useful, its shelf life was destined to be short. Each piece in this set is clearly marked underneath with a label detailing the designers, the model and the maker.
£800 (table and chair set)

'DENIM WARE'

Designer jeans were certainly taking the world of fashion by storm, so it's no wonder that 'Denim Ware' found a place on the table. The range (c.1978) was another bright idea from Carlton Ware (est. 1890) who took their lead from street style and 'Jean Genie' fashion for denim worn with cheesecloth shirts. Yet despite Carlton's great hopes for their up-to-the-minute tableware, its appeal was short-lived. This means that you will have to hunt around in order to find pieces today. Those who did buy Denim Ware tended to go for a mug or a tea plate rather then the optional milk jug, which is as a relative rarity today. **£20-30 (salt and pepper) £10-15 (tea plate) £25-30 (milk jug) £20-25 (mug)**

'WALKING WARE'

The colourful striped socks and strapped shoes on British pottery Carlton Ware's appealing 'Walking Ware' would have stood out a mile on any dining table. The series was the combined effort of husband and wife team, Roger Mitchell and Danka Napiorkowska who developed the idea in their own pottery ('Lustre') before linking with Carlton Ware to mass-produce the range from 1973. Walking Ware may be fun, frivolous and a little bit kitsch but there's a loyal gang of fans out there who will do anything to get hold of it. Egg cups and cups are fairly easily found but plates are not. They were made in three sizes (small, medium and large) and all are rare. Those feet had a habit of snapping so watch for repairs and check for the Carlton Ware factory mark on the bottom. **£8 (egg cup) £15 (cup) £120 (plate)**

MIDWINTER 'STYLE'

Midwinter pottery's 'Style' designed by Eve Midwinter (the founder's grand-daughter) in 1983 was a clear move away from that rugged, natural look that had dominated seventies ceramic design. Pastel colours decorated a shape that can only be described as delicate giving it a real feminine feel (mirrored by flouncy high street fashions and New Romantic pop music). Conveniently dual-purpose, it was branded a 'beverage dispenser' because it doubled as a tea and coffee pot. In collectors' terms it's a newcomer, but dispensers like these in pristine condition are relatively rare because of their less than practical design. Unless you positioned it correctly the lid dropped inside and the basket handle was prone to snapping. Many haven't stood the test of time so perfect pieces are sought after. **£30+**

MENDINI CANDLESTICK

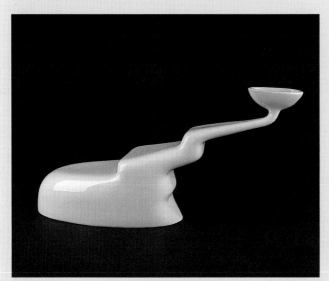

When Italian designer-architect Alessandro Mendini (b.1931) decided to style a candlestick, he came up with this – for Italian manufacturer Zanotta's 'Zabro' collection in 1985. The fact that its stepped asymmetric outline isn't exactly conventional is typical of his work for Studio Alchimia (the Italian design group he helped to establish in 1976). By concentrating on elaborate decoration Mendini and the group flouted those who judged good design on form and function alone. Like Alchimia's other work, Mendini's candlestick was very much anti-design. Early pieces from the seventies are cherished because many were exhibition one-offs intended to make a point. Later vases like this were made in larger runs but nothing like mass market numbers, which means they're still period rarities. Look for the moulded 'Zabro' mark underneath. **£130**

KNOLL'S 'QUEEN ANNE'

Dining in a truly modern way was something American architect-designer, Robert Venturi (b.1925) achieved with this range of furniture for US furniture maker, Knoll. Launched in May 1984, he broke fresh ground by creating a modern style from a blend of new and old. At the time, Venturi talked about his furniture crossing 'the boundary between tradition and modern design by adapting a series of historical styles to industrial processes. It also uses symbolism and decoration but in a modern way.' Those who plumped for Venturi's design had a choice of aptly named historical styles like this one titled 'Queen Anne'. **£150+ each**

HOVIS WARE'

By the mid-eighties, Hovis (named in 1890) was Britain's most famous bread brand. So when the Carlton Ware pottery launched their Hovis breakfast set (c. 1983), they were sure of success. Unfortunately, they had failed to seek permission from Rank Hovis Ltd (makers of the loaf), who frowned upon the first few pieces (a toast rack, butter dish and mug). By 1985 Rank Hovis officially sanctioned the Carlton Ware range that sold in high street stores including Habitat. It is these eighties pieces with their distinctive 'burnt toast' look and 'Carlton Ware' mark in the distinctive uppercase typeface, which are more collectable than nineties revivals marked with a script signature.

£15-20 (toast rack) £30-40 (butter dish) £30-40 (mug) £35-40 (plate) £60-80 (teapot)

'HONEYCOMB'

In 1986 an enterprising group of new directors rescued England's great art pottery, Moorcroft (founded 1913) from the doldrums. Flagging sales at Moorcroft were partly due to the fact that no new major designs had been issued for over a decade. So the new team, headed by Chairman Hugh Edwards, started to revive Moorcroft's fortunes with a run of fresh ranges. 'Honeycomb', designed by Philip Richardson was one of the first, but its unusually short lifespan (1987-89) means it's a rarity now. Because it was way ahead of its time with its appealing use of honeybees, retailers were nervous. The public, they claimed, wouldn't want to see stinging insects on their tableware, so shop orders and displays were minimized. It's not surprising that fewer than 1,000 pieces of 'Honeycomb' actually sold. The ginger jar (bottom right) is the most sought-after in the range. Then it was priced at £60 - now it's worth more nearly ten times that amount! **£550(large vase, top right) £400 (smaller vase, top left) £500 (urn vase, centre) £500 (ginger jar, bottom right) £210 (covered dish, bottom left)**

'MEMPHIS' VASE

The bright colours and eclectic style of this 'Euphrates' vase (1983) are a big clue to its maker, the influential designer-architect Ettore Sottsass (b.1917). It's another gem from the Memphis Group who made such a big impact on interiors world-wide throughout the eighties. The key to finding a new design style, they believed, was in juxtapositioning a spectrum of colours and forms like you'd never seen before. Shocking, fun and exciting, the Memphis-look meant whatever you wanted it to. But the main thing was that it was free from design dogma and took a fresh direction. Inspiration came from fifties and sixties popular culture. The interiors of bars and cafes with their Formica topped surfaces had already caught Sottsass' eye. Mixed in with that was a reverence to the art and architecture of ancient Egypt (hence the Group's name, Memphis, the site of the vast Royal cemetery). **£575**

VILLEROY & BOCH

While Italian style was busy influencing our living space, American style was hard at work everywhere else. Britain in the eighties saw a boom in fast-food restaurants and out of town satellite superstores. Town dwellers were treated to versions of Manhattan-style loft living and the American trend was spreading across Europe. So it's no wonder that the German ceramics firm, Villeroy & Boch (founded 1748) chose the 'Spirit of the USA' as a theme for their new range of tableware. They commissioned talented design students from Vienna's Academy of Applied Arts to craft tableware that embodied those all-American values. Young Klara Obereder came up with this 'Coca-Cola' set in 1988 – a tableware range that drew its shape and design from the Coca-Cola bottle, – an icon of the twentieth century. At the time, Germany was on the road to re-unification and Coca-Cola stood for unity. Appealing to both Coca-Cola collectors (who number many thousands) and eighties style fans, this set is sought-after, especially when you realise that only fifty were ever made. **£1,500-1,800 (the set)**

MELAMINE

Melamine re-appeared in the eighties, not as the new wonder material this time, but as the plastic that would last longer than any ceramic, so saving on precious natural resources. American housewares manufacturer Copco brought in New York design team Smart Design to create a range of products to show just how versatile plastic could be at home. This brightly coloured dinnerware set was something they came up with in 1987. It fitted perfectly with the general mood, poking fun at the purity of the Post-Modern look with it's randomly decorated plates. **£50**

BRANZI TABLE

Italian architect-designer, Andrea Branzi (b.1938) explored a new direction in dining with this table. Instead of just looks, eighties clients were treated to a sensory riot. Not only were the colours a fantastic visual stimuli but the mixture of materials (burr yew veneer for the top, metal for the base and roughly finished silver birch branches for the legs) cried out to be touched. This inspired interpretation of anti-design was unveiled to the world at the 'Domestic Animals Exhibition' in Milan, 1985. As a collector's piece today, it's a dining table of importance in terms of eighties style – doubly revered because this was one of the actual pieces shown at the exhibition. **£3,000-4,000**

'OYSTER' CHAIR

A dining chair for the future with a bit of nostalgia woven in. British architect, Nigel Coates's (b. 1949) 'Oyster' chair made its first public appearance in his futuristic 'Oyster House', a new-style home for the next millennium, which was voted 'Concept House '98' at the 1998 *Daily Mail* Ideal Home Exhibition. At a glance it seems just as modern as the home it was intended for with its structure pared down to the bare minimum for open-plan living. But take a closer look at the seat and there's something comfortingly familiar. It's a clever re-working of thirties Lloyd Loom, woven from the same classic twisted paper strands as granny's armchair. Hardly a surprise when you realize that Coates has collaborated with Lloyd Loom of Spalding Ltd to make it. It's already been plucked out as an example of creative British design thanks to the influential Powerhouse::UK exhibition (1998) so the 'Oyster' chair is sitting pretty as far as potential goes. **£185+**

'TOAST AND MARMALADE'

Emma Bridgewater's (b.1960) 'Toast and Marmalade' series has captured the nineties mood just as Clarice Cliff did with her vibrant 'Bizarre' tablewares back in the thirties. Emma Bridgewater launched her instantly recognizable range in 1992, offering a fresh approach to eating that cleverly cut across age and gender boundaries. Her choice of words as decoration instead of a conventional pattern (inspired by Suffragette Movement china from the turn of the century) broadened its appeal. Whether you're young or old, a bachelor or a housewife, a connoisseur or a layman, 'Toast and Marmalade' fits – probably the reason why it's still her best-selling line. Success has bred imitators so do check each piece carries the printed 'Bridgewater' mark.
£10.95 (8½ inch 'Toast and Marmalade' plate)
£7.95 (egg cup)
£29.95 (cup and saucer)

'CITY' CUTLERY

David Mellor's (b. 1930) sublimely modern 'City' cutlery takes eating tools into a new realm – the third dimension. Only by harnessing the very latest computer technology has the 1998 'City' range been able to be something more than a series of dream sketches. Sophisticated welding techniques are used to manufacture the precision moulded handles – a key feature of Mellor's revolutionary new styling. What you get is a real depth of design and a feel of solidity and substance from the moment you pick up a piece. 'I wanted to make shapes more ergonomically correct for the hand when eating,' says Mellor. All crucial criteria when it comes to food tools. With the great Mellor name behind it and the 'City' branding, this cutlery could well yield a bonus in the future!

£71.50 (for a six-piece setting)

'CONRAN COLLECTION'

'A collection dedicated to providing the very best modern products for the home' is how Terence Conran describes his 'Conran Collection' (launched 1997). Each one of the 1,000 products selected to carry the distinctive own-brand CC symbol (a dissected target mark) like these glasses, is exclusive to the Group and shows the talents of their in-house Conran Design Partnership (est. 1993). These are the designs that are plucked out and held up high as 'benchmarks of quality, manufacture, design and function'. So buy them, years from now we'll cherish these pieces as nineties style leaders.

£4.95-6.95 (glasses)

EMMA O'DARE GLASSWARE

Up-and-coming glass maker Emma O'Dare (b.1972) uses the pâte-de-verre technique that was popularized by French glassmakers Daum and Argy-Rousseau earlier this century. But this time she gives it a contemporary twist by mixing ceramic oxides with powdered recycled glass. The result is truly inspirational with deep sea-blue colouring and a texture that begs to be handled. So far she's been singled out as one of Britain's best glass talents by the Crafts Council and with pieces like this bowl she's set to go far. **£680**

KEITH HARING TABLEWARE

It seems odd to see what was once New York's underground graffiti art emblazoned on some of the finest tableware money can buy. But contemporary American artist Keith Haring's (1958-90) doodle-like paintings shot to fame and respectability because of their instantly recognisable images. 'Art gains power through imagination, invention, and confrontation,' said Haring and private collectors and museums, aroused by his call, snapped up his work, complete with its deep underlying messages. This 'Spirit of Art' coffee set made by German ceramics giant, Villeroy & Boch (founded 1748), honoured Haring who had sadly died before it appeared in 1991. The link with the great man himself is important enough, but Villeroy & Boch sealed the success of this set by only making 500. This one still has its original packaging. **£2,000-2,500**

'MISS TRIP' CHAIR

From toothbrushes and scooters to an Olympic Flame and furniture for the former French President, the late Francois Mitterrand's, private apartment at the Elysée Palace, there is very little that great French designer, Philippe Starck (b.1949), hasn't tackled. His designs are legendary, and apart from over-all good looks and classy styling you can hardly forget something with an off-beat name like 'Mister Bliss' or 'Bubu'. With Starck, objects have personalities and that's reinforced with his string of baffling titles. This chair ('Miss Trip') is no exception. Lovable because it's so practical he draws on the successful self-assembly formula by presenting his creation in parts. Like all good take-aways you get a box filled with the bits and pieces you need to assemble the chair. And once Miss Trip's made the journey home and been put together (conveniently avoiding lengthy delivery time) she's a truly stylish piece of design, combining beech wood for the frame with a polypropylene seat. Inevitably it's going to be the still boxed versions that will be valuable gems years from now. **£149.90**

MOORCROFT'S 'COBRIDGE'

When Moorcroft's new Phoenix Works in Stoke-on-Trent cracked the century-old secret of decorating high-fired stoneware with their famous Cobridge range, the ceramics world was rocked. Nothing like it had appeared for decades and it was heralded as a real triumph when it was launched in October 1998. Predictably, retailers and Moorcroft collectors are already scrambling for vases like this one with its classic image of Staffordshire's famous bottle kilns – such a feature of Britain's industrial landscape a century ago. **£230**

MALLELIEU TEAPOT

The individual organic style and luxuriously rich glaze of this teapot gives tea drinking a sense of ceremony. Studio ceramics are booming as serious modern collectables and its maker, British potter Fenella Mallelieu (b. 1956) could well be classed as the next Lucie Rie. There's the same emotional response to colour and a real feel for and understanding of her material – clay. Add to that her pedigree of excellence, training at Goldsmith's College (à la Damien Hurst) plus prize-winning in the V&A's 'Ceramic Contemporaries' show, and you've got a winner. No wonder the V&A have been quietly buying Fenella's pots for their permanent collection. **£85**

TRANSGLASS

If you've ever wondered where your old wine bottles end up, it could well be here. Encouraged by exhibitions like the Crafts Council's 'Recycling: Forms for the Next Century' in 1996, designers have started to explore reusing materials to save the world's dwindling natural resources. These water carafes, jugs and vases started life on supermarket shelves filled with wine and beer. Reincarnated, they've become designers Transglass's (the London-based partnership of Emma Woffenden (b.1962) and Tord Boontje (b.1968)) 'Bottle Collection'. Here, simple cutting and soft polishing techniques have achieved a really fresh look for throw-away materials. Be sure it's the real thing by looking for the makers' small enamel 'Transglass' mark on the bottom of each piece. Already plucked out as key pieces of British Design in the 1998 Powerhouse::UK show it won't be long before Tranglass's Bottle Collection is considered too precious to use. **£10 (drinking glass) £35 (jug) £40 (vase)**

IN THE
Bedroom

PIFCO Hairdryer

Dries hair really fast — turns hair-drying from a lengthy chore into a short, pleasant interlude.

The motor — the most powerful of its kind — dries the thickest hair in a matter of minutes; dries it perfectly, carefully, quickly. The beautifully balanced plastic casing has a particularly pleasing shape and is available in a choice of colours — Petal Pink, Pastel Blue, Maple Green, Lilac and Ivory. 'On-Off' and 'Hot-Cold' switches built into the comfortable handgrip give fingertip control. Universal A.C./D.C. motor with self aligning bearings is fully suppressed against radio and T.V. interference. Loading: 50 watts cold; 550 watts hot. Six feet flex and adaptor fitted.

The attractive Red and Gold presentation box adds the finishing touch to the Pifco Hairdryer — the perfect gift. Awarded the Good Housekeeping Seal of Merit.

No. 1050/4703   For 200/250 volts.   63/-
11/6 Tax

74/6 Complete

In 1952 the Utility Scheme, which had dictated fashion for over a decade, finally came to an end. Nowhere was the sense of relief felt so keenly as in the bedroom. The days when wardrobes were filled with rugged economy-cut suits, branded with CC41 labels were over. The fifties ushered in a new style of women's dressing, symbolized by ultra-feminine cuts, glorious accessories and no skimping on luxurious materials.

French couturier, Christian Dior, triumphed with his hourglass outline, paving the way for Marilyn Monroe's shapely figure and teetering stilettos. Dior's couture was strictly for the moneyed classes, however it was not long before ready-to-wear copies appeared in the average housewife's wardrobe. The department store dresses that she saved for were machine-stitched in crease resistant fabrics.

A flurry of synthetics – nylon, rayon, terylene and polyester, as well as improved natural fibres like the 'fabulous Shan-su', a drip-dry, silk look-alike actually made from cotton appeared. Against a backdrop of multiplying electrical appliances, especially washing machines, modern easy-care fabrics were ideal. They were also easy to print, meaning that they could keep pace with changing teenage fashions.

With the arrival of the 'swinging' sixties, teenage style really took hold. Instead of 'the look' filtering down from couture exclusives, as it had done a decade before, it rose up from the young 'revolution' on the streets. London was a hotbed of fashion boutiques and Mary Quant's 'Bazaar' was the place to go for Mod outfits. Her quest was to 'make fashionable clothes available to everyone' and hangers across the land were draped with Quant-inspired, tights, mini skirts and dresses, made from the 'Space Age' materials of the day – orlon, courtelle, crimplene and PVC. The widespread availability of the Pill and the spread of pop music stimulated a general feeling of self-assertiveness in female style.

For girls, cosmetics had a major role to play in creating the right image. Realizing this, manufacturers used advertising to target the youth market with exciting new products. With aspirations to look like Britain's sylph-like model, Twiggy and TV's cult pop presenter Cathy McGowan, it's no wonder that tubed mascara (rather than blocked) and easy-stick false eyelashes were such a hit.

But fashion wasn't just for women. The 'Peacock Revolution' was afoot in the sixties, hailing a flamboyant style of dressing for men that centred on London's fashionable Carnaby Street. Teenage boys idolized the pop groups who shopped there – the Beatles, the Kinks and the Rolling Stones. Bedecked in polo necks, brightly printed shirts and waisted jackets they followed their heroes' every move and adopted their psychedelic and openly unisex style of dressing.

A decade later, the lines between male and female fashion were totally blurred. Jeans (albeit designer labelled and flared) were commonplace for both men and women, while bell-bottomed trouser suits for the independent woman encroached upon what was traditionally considered male executive tailoring.

As the seventies progressed, the pendulum of style swung from the romantic flowing lines and maxi-lengths found in Biba's High Street Kensington emporium, through glam rock's pointed polyester and platforms to end with the radical subversive styles that became Punk. At the heart of this anti-chic style was British designer, Vivienne Westwood, who with Sex Pistols manager, Malcolm McLaren, became a real *tour de force* in the new movement, which revolved around a series of extraordinary shops (from 'Sex' to 'Seditionaries') on London's King's Road.

By the eighties, fashion had switched direction once again. In 1981, Westwood signified a new style with her 'Pirate' collection, full of voluminous printed shirts and fantasy. New Romantic pop music adopted the look and fans, hungry for a style of their own, followed suit. Designers like Katharine Hamnett believed that what you wore conveyed your views to the world. Her high-profile printed T-shirts are hard to forget because they tackled the issues of the day with provocative slogans.

In the office it was slick power-dressing that counted. Inspired by weekly doses of American TV soaps like *Dallas* and *Dynasty* square-cut, shoulder-padded suits became acceptable apparel for both sexes. For the status conscious, the image was completed by a limited edition Swatch wristwatch on display just below the cuff.

By the nineties the hard-working female executives of the eighties were ready to redefine their femininity and the world of fashion was on hand to help. Simple, shapely cuts in luxurious fabrics from Brit-pack designers like Matthew Williamson, gave women a softer outline. Embroidered and sequinned decoration added a note of glamour whilst traditional accessories; hats, handbags and jewellery played on the notion of a beautiful young coquette.

in the bedroom

VOGUE MAGAZINE

After the regimented styles and fabrics of wartime – thanks to the Board of Trade's Utility Scheme (1941-52) – it was light relief to flick through the pages of British *Vogue*. Slim-waisted, full-skirted, 'New Look' dresses, in sumptuous materials took the world by storm in 1947, when they were paraded in Christian Dior's (1905-57) salon show. However, these were exclusive, expensive couture pieces and it was left to fashion magazines like Condé Nast's *Vogue* (first seen in America in 1892, Britain in 1916 and France in the twenties) to give those who could stretch to the three shilling cover price their first taste of post-war glamour. This run of British issues from 1950 tended to carry the same covers as the equivalent US editions, although there was about a third less reading material, because the Utility Scheme was still up and running. Classic photographers like Irving Penn and Cecil Beaton were drafted in to magic these dreamy covers, which signalled a new era in fashion and photography. To show things were changing *Vogue* even ran a feature on 'The Rise of Ready to Wear'. And the *Vogue* Pattern Service (est. 1905) did their bit to make high-style more accessible with the launch of their exclusive 'Paris Original Models' – a new series of home-sew patterns inspired by couture fashions. Today both *Vogue* magazines and their original sewing patterns from the fifties are prized for their period comment – the less dog-eared, the better.

£10-15 each (*Vogue* magazines)
£5 each (*Vogue* patterns)

DRESSING TABLE

Italian designers take the credit for much of the fifties modern look. Thanks to key players like architect/designer Giovanni Ponti (1891-1979), their innovative styling even found its way into the bedroom. This dressing table, made by Dassi around 1954/55, proved just how well the wonder plastic laminate, Formica, worked outside the kitchen when it was mixed with traditional woods – in this case oak. Its pared down tapering legs are a marked contrast to the heavy, dark wood pre-war designs. The offset mirror wasn't simply a practical consideration – it was Ponti's way of counteracting the overall regularity of the piece, thus showing that he was in tune with the fifties fascination for asymmetry. *Domus* magazine (founded 1928), which Ponti edited, was the bible for modern interior style and regular *Domus*-Formica competitions encouraged furniture designers to incorporate new plastic surfacing materials into their work. So, it's no surprise to see this dressing table featured in the magazine's 1956 Christmas edition.

£800-1,200

GOBLIN TEAMADE

British engineer, Brenner Thornton, invented this design classic, the Goblin Teasmade, in 1936. With fewer, if any, servants in the home after the war the automatic tea-maker came into its own. In the early days a sceptical public needed reassurance from the retailers who were often heard to say, 'No Madam, it's not the work of the Devil.' But by the fifties its virtues were really appreciated. 'How to give him his morning tea – and still play the sleeping beauty,' said the adverts. The advantage with the Goblin models, whose styling changed to suit furnishing trends, was that as well as a 'superb' tea-maker it doubled as a light and an electric clock – 'space-saving combination'. No wonder teasmades were given away in their hundreds as prizes for TV and radio's new quiz shows. The curvaceous styling of this model ran throughout the fifties and into the sixties. As collectors' items they must be pristine (no cracks or chips in the teapot, which should be original – check it fits), the original plastic serving tray is important and finding the china sold with it (in the 'Queen Anne' Gift) is a bonus. Check the surface carefully, Goblins were often painted or even wallpapered to match their bedroom setting! **£30-50**

HAIR GRIPS

There was no surer way of selling your product than getting it endorsed by the stars. Few women could resist the suave looks of Hollywood actor Gregory Peck (b. 1916) after *Roman Holiday* (1953) or the perfect smile of British crooner, Dickie Valentine and even hair grip firms took advantage of it. Sales of grips boomed during the fifties after hair rollers were launched early on in the decade. British actress, Eunice Grayson, star of *The Revenge of Frankenstein* (1958) appeared on Newey's 'Blend Rite' packet sporting the new fashionable style – shorter hair with controlled curls, teased and held in place with spray. It's unusual to find unused packets and even rarer to see the printed shots of Peck and Valentine still intact – smitten fans usually cut out the photographs to carry in their purses!
£2-3 (Blend Rite grips) £4 (Starlite and Top Note grips)

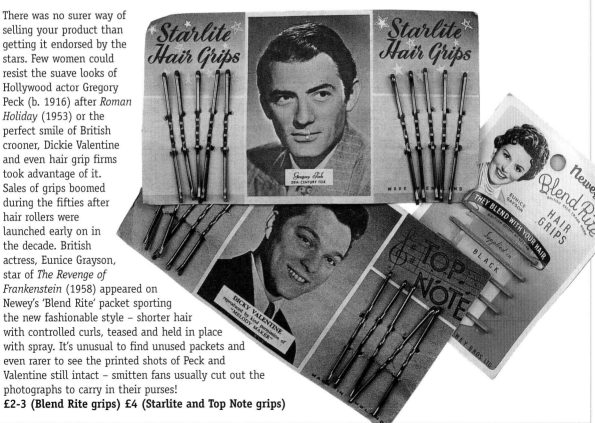

MARTINI SKIRT

Teenagers who jived to the hit sounds of Rock 'n' Roll in cinema aisles and dance halls demanded their own distinctive upbeat look to set them apart from their parents. For girls, a full circle (or dirndl) skirt like this was a must with a matching wide belt, tight-fitting polo-neck jersey or scoop-necked top and flat-soled pumps (known as 'flatties'). Competition was intense as they bunched up their hair in ponytails and donned make-up to stand out from the crowd. When it came to fashion, it was the brightest, most striking designs that counted – not to mention the number of paper nylon or stiffened net petticoats you wore underneath. The Martini Rossi label on this skirt was instantly recognisable and ultra chic, fitting with the fifties fondness for cocktails.

£50-70

PIFCO HAIRDRYER

Weekly trips to hairdressing salons to keep the curls in place may have been good for gossip but they were expensive. Electrical firms responded to the thousands of housewives who desperately wanted to create the same look cheaply at home. This fashion pastel hairdryer from British electrical firm, Pifco (founded 1936), was one of the decade's most popular dryers, designed to match their 'famous' vibratory massager. Launched in 1950 it was a slimmed-down version of their solid pre-war Bakelite models. Countless Pifco adverts promoted the dryer as a must-have essential because the 'drying time was cut down by more than half'. Then there was the bonus of its attractive packaging (a gold box with an aluminium badge) – proof of Pifco quality that won this model a *Good Housekeeping* Seal of Merit, making it 'the perfect gift'. Those who could afford the 74s 6d price tag could rest assured they could still tune in to their favourite programme because this model was 'TV and radio suppressed' – although sheer motor noise meant the set would have to be on full volume! Look out for the rare cream and red version.

£10-25 (boxed) £50 (cream/red)

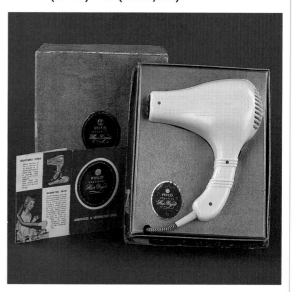

SUNGLASSES

These sunglasses were *the* stylish fifties accessories to own. They gave the wearer the opportunity to look like Grace Kelly, Doris Day or Brigitte Bardot – all screen-idols, who were captured on newsreels hiding behind dark-tinted glasses to avoid the glare of publicity. The distinctly pointed shape went with the fashionable 'doe-eyed' make-up look, where eyeliner was drawn out to a point to emphasize the eyes. **£15-20**

DRESSES

From ultra-expensive to modestly affordable, these were the day dresses that spanned fifties wardrobes. At the top end was the immensely talented and influential Parisian couturier, Christian Dior (1905-57), whose tiny waists and billowing skirts revived the whole notion of femininity. This ivory organza dress (right) with its tightly fitted bodice and shawl collar is typical of Dior's tailoring at the very beginning of the fifties. No skimping on materials here, the full skirt uses yards of stiff net petticoat to hold its shape and mixes cheap raffia (a plant fibre

native to Madagascar), with the very finest lace and beads for the exquisitely embroidered floral pattern. But all this attention to detail came at a price that was way beyond the average pocket. However, thanks to enterprising manufacturers and technological breakthroughs like fully mechanized screen-printing and easy-care synthetics, the 'New Look' hit the high street. Coloured cottons quickly and cheaply responded to fifties motifs bringing the latest styles within everyone's reach. 'Cotton has never been

prettier' announced *Vogue*, although synthetic fabrics tried hard to compete. Flower motifs were enduringly popular and London-based Victor Josselyn's blue cotton cocktail dress from the late fifties has a hint of romance, with its printed long-stemmed roses. All you needed to complete the look was a padded bra or some 'falsies' to accentuate the fashionably pointed bustline.
£800-1,500 (Dior) £50-80 (Josselyn)

ELECTRIC DRY RAZOR

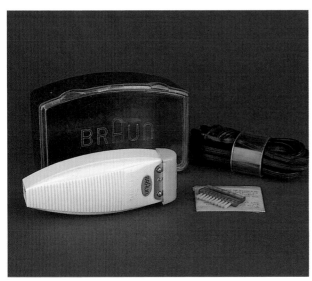

For the modern man who wanted 'the finest, closest, and most perfect shave' an electric dry shaver – the sort of thing so famously used by James Stewart in Hitchcock's *Rear Window* (1954) – was the ideal gadget. German electrical giant, Braun's R&D team designed this S.50 model, taking over where Max Braun had left off during the war. Launched in 1950, it was the first Braun shaver to have an oscillating cutting block, which was covered by a very thin but tough steel foil screen. To us, this technology seems boringly standard but in the fifties it was as fresh as the cream plastic case it was wrapped up in. However, Braun made sure they appealed to the traditionalists, by offering the same model in black plastic. As you can see, its styling was smooth like the shave it promised and the S.50 was astonishingly compact and light. That made it ideal for travel – hence the dual voltage (110/240V) switch on the back. For the growing body of razor collectors and design gurus an S.50 is a must. **£40-50**

THE KELLY BAG

Hollywood actresses had a big impact on women's fashions and were effectively classed as the Supermodels of their day. Grace Kelly (1928-82) was so influential as a style leader that she even lent her name to a handbag – 'The Kelly Bag'. Both on and off screen Kelly was styled as little short of perfect; she was naturally beautiful, with a warm personality and a real sense of elegance when it came to dressing. No wonder the French leather specialist, Hermés (founded 1837) renamed a bag they'd first made in the thirties, in Kelly's honour, twenty years on. Today the stylish image still persists and a waiting list for new Kelly bags (priced at up to £9,000) means that there is plenty of interest in vintage fifties editions. Watch out for clever copies. Apart from the hallmark padlock the inside of the real thing is stamped 'HERMÉS PARIS'.
£800-2,000

BRYLCREEM

It wasn't just teenage girls who strove to look different. Young boys still living at home rebelled in their own way with slicked back hair and quiffs, which their idols, Elvis Presley, James Dean and Marlon Brando, would have been proud of. Even though they thought that they were being modern, it's interesting that they turned to their father's cupboard for help. Because full sheen 'Brylcreem' guaranteed to 'make your hair look excitingly clean – and disturbingly healthy' had been around since the thirties. With advertising jingles in the United States like 'Brylcreem, the gals will all pursue ya – They'll love to get their fingers in your hair', it is really no wonder so many youngsters clamoured to use it!
£5

YVES SAINT LAURENT

Although a desirable 'Christian Dior' label is sewn into the back of this head-turning outfit it was actually designed after Dior's death by his young successor, Yves Saint Laurent (b. 1936). Following in the footsteps of such a great designer was never going to be easy. However, this superbly tailored dress and matching cropped box jacket from the 1959 Autumn-Winter collection, showed Saint Laurent had plenty of flair himself. His A-line dress wasn't bolstered with a complicated support system of boning and padding that had been such a feature of Dior's early designs. In fact, it was a much freer affair with the shape moulded by a network of darts, giving a feel of what was to come. Saint Laurent's reign at Dior lasted for just two years before he was called away for National Service. So, for collectors this is a key early ensemble (in pristine condition) that really shows his talent. Bidding went sky high recently when it popped up at auction. The modest £600 estimate got left behind as Yves Saint Laurent himself, determined to buy back a piece of his own history, paid a great deal more. **£25,000**

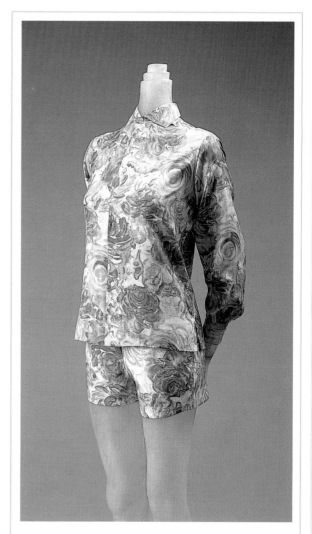

PLAY SUIT

This lime-green playsuit was one of the typically fun outfits from Italian designer, Emilio Pucci (1914-92). A natty ensemble, it appeared in 1958, the year that BOAC (British Overseas Airways Corporation) launched the world's first transatlantic jet service. The fifties witnessed a boom in commercial air travel and new 'Tourist Class' seats on some airlines paved the way for the package holidays to come. But flying was still prohibitively expensive and those that did take to the air were undeniably rich. They were the kind of clientele who indulged in Pucci's brightly printed and luxuriously silky garments, which not only looked good but were handy for travellers too. Take ten of these for the beach and they folded up to nothing in a suitcase. Early outfits are simply labelled, whilst later Pucci (from the sixties and seventies) also has his distinctive 'Emilio' signature intertwined in the fabric's pattern. **£250-350**

in the bedroom

DISPOSABLE A-LINE MINIS

Disposable sixties fashions were perfect for 'entertaining, lounging, travelling and shopping'! But however fun an A-line 'paper' mini dress like this was to wear, it was a symbol of the throwaway society it was made for. Consumerism was booming, as an expanding number of self-service supermarkets offered a wider choice of mass market products, rival brands fought advertising wars, and the shopper took home a basket of quick-cook, easy-keep meals. Those stoic ideas of wartime thrift and 'make do and mend' gave way to the notion of 'here today, gone tomorrow'. American Pop artist, Andy Warhol (1928-87) was one of those who saw consumerism as both a blessing and a nightmare. While his famous painting, '200 Campbell's Soup Cans' (1962), found its way on to disposable paper 'souper' dresses, American card firm, Hallmark Cards Inc (est. 1910) made 'Flower Fantasy' versions like this. In this case, the 'paper' is actually a mixture of cellulose with a little nylon added for stretch. Conveniently, it was sized but the length you wore it was optional – simply 'shorten with scissors' read the instructions. Most were worn once and simply consigned to the bin (or burnt if you stood too near an open fire!). This means that any surviving dresses are unusual, especially if unopened. **£150**

MARY QUANT BOOTS

British designer, Mary Quant (b. 1934), launched these Quant Afoot ankle boots to go with her wet-look PVC range. Quant was the first designer to really capitalize on the short 'n' sweet look that epitomized 'Swinging London' and actually wore a mini-skirt to Buckingham Palace to collect her OBE. 'The whole point of fashion is to make clothes available to everyone,' explained Quant and she gave girls what they wanted. Like her clothes, Quant's rainboots are easy to spot because of the hallmark daisy – here it's stamped on the heel. **£100**

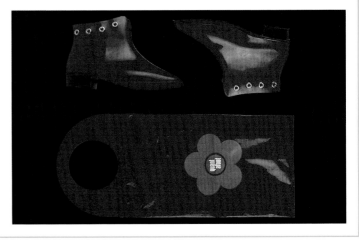

CARNABY STREET

Fashion in the sixties wasn't exclusively female. Young men too responded to the sound of the Kinks' lyrics ('A dedicated follower of fashion'), the buzz of Carnaby Street and the relaxed look of The Beatles in their 1965 movie, *Help*. So the 'Peacock Revolution' amongst the scooter brigade was afoot, and designers like Emilio Pucci were ready to cater for the affluent style-conscious male clientele who would happily spend £5–6 a week on a pair of shoes or a shirt. The undisputed 'King' of Carnaby Street, where affordable sixties high style erupted, was John Stephen who at one time had nine thriving shops there – a Mecca for stars like the Beatles, Herman (from Herman's Hermits) and The Rolling Stones. This psychedelic kipper tie would have hung in one of his boutiques around the time of The Summer of Love (1967). Like this tailored jacket, which was sold a few doors down in Carnaby Street's 'Kleptomania', traditional Indian chintz and paisley motifs were a major influence. 'Exotic fashions from far away places have been appearing in the shops more and more,' reported *Woman's Own* in 1969. And along with a growing interest in the teachings of Maharishi Mahesh Yogi who entertained the Beatles, Mike Love of the Beach Boys and Mia Farrow at his refuge in the Himalayan foothills, India and all things ethnic were 'in' by the end of the decade.

£10-15 (tie)
£200-300 (jacket)

STOCKINGS V TIGHTS

By the mid-sixties the rising hemline of the mini-skirt posed a problem. Traditional stockings and garters were the mainstay of women's fashion but the mini threatened to reveal all. It was Mary Quant who realised that tights, traditionally worn by dancers, could be stylish accessories for the street with a built-in sense of decency! Stocking manufacturers were forced to compete with Quant's tights in vivid colours and varied patterns. Teenage girls were enticed to buy these lacy purple stockings because of the young fun scooter picture on the backing card. As you can imagine, it's unusual to find a packet that hasn't been opened.

£5 (stockings in original packaging – the same value for a pair of unopened Quant tights)

FALSE EYELASHES

False eyelashes were vital fashion accessories in this decade. Mary Quant's lashes, introduced as part of her make-up line, could be cut down and tailor-made to suit the wearer. An unopened boxed set like this is an appealing extra for collectors of Quant clothes. **£5**

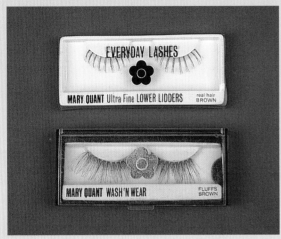

TALCUM POWDER

Margot of Mayfair were sure of sales with their Beatles talcum powder. Images of the clean-cut 'Fab Four' had instant appeal and no self-respecting female fan could survive without talc like this. Most were eagerly used and thrown away and it's unusual to find one that's unopened. **£150-200**

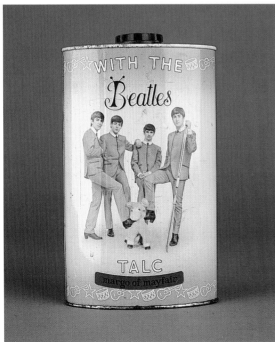

CARDIN JUMPER DRESS

The riot of plastics, PVC and metallic vinyl, that dominated sixties fashion was fitting for a world preoccupied with the Space Programme. From the designer that gave the Beatles their collarless suits in 1963 (Pierre Cardin, b. 1922) came this 'Space Age' jumper dress (1968/69). The central patent leather brace was one of his hallmarks but instead of mixing it with sheer fabrics, favoured by other designers, Cardin chose figure-hugging ribbed jersey. Similarly, it was the androgynous look that counted in the shape of Vidal Sassoon's boyish cropped 'Kwan' haircut (as worn by Nancy Kwan – star of the sixties east meets west romance, *The World of Susie Wong*), model Twiggy's flat profile and trouser suits. The micro-miniskirt line was symptomatic of the widespread confusion that swamped the closing years of the decade. Social and political turmoil in the late sixties spread into the world of fashion blurring the lines of what was considered stylish. So you'd be just as likely to see an 'It' girl wearing this super-short outfit with high boots and a maxi-length coat. **£600-700**

DRESS & COAT

This tango orange dress and coat was styled by the chief designer at the House of Dior, Marc Bohan (b.1926) in 1966 – the same year that his Doctor Zhivago collection (inspired by the hit 1965 film) was shown. Bohan was known for cleverly adapting the 'Swinging Sixties' street fashions for his more select couture clientele. The 'little girl lost' look was popularized by the waif-thin model, Lesley Hornby, (known around the world as 'Twiggy') and on screen by Sue Lyon as the teenage temptress 'Lolita Haze,' in Stanley Kubrick's film *Lolita*, 1962. Bohan used a flat-fronted two-tone bodice and 'gym-slip' skirt to give it a real schoolgirl feel. The hand-written labels sewn inside both garments with the customer's name show they were couture pieces, which adds to their importance and value. The prêt-à-porter (ready-to-wear) versions would have been more modestly priced and are consequently less valuable today. **£800-1,200**

in the bedroom

PUNK FASHION

In the same way that the Mods and Rockers turned to dress to signify their youthful defiance in the sixties, bored working-class teenagers a decade later swooped on anti-establishment Punk fashion. Bands like the Damned, the Sex Pistols and the Clash were these teenagers' idols. And the artificially torn, stained, safety-pinned and chained Punk look they wore found mass appeal, thanks to shops like 'Seditionaries' (a Vivienne Westwood-Malcolm McLaren venture) and the 'Boy' boutique (run by Stephane Raynor and John Kirvine). These outlets on London's King's Road became the Mecca for youths with dyed, spiked hair who wore red, black and white to stand out. This Destroy T-shirt (right) was dreamed up by Westwood, McLaren and their art director, Jamie Reid, for sale in 'Seditionaries'. You could hardly fail to notice it because of the street images and slogans that were contrasted to shock. As its wearer remembers, 'Punk was an experience – you didn't wear it to behave – you wore it to misbehave!' which is why Punk originals in good condition are in such short supply and snapped up by collectors today. As well as the trademark 'Seditionaries' label sewn on the outer sleeve, the words printed beneath the Swastika are the famed lyrics from the Sex Pistols' debut single 'Anarchy in the UK' (1976) – the link being Malcolm McLaren who was also their manager. These tight-legged tartan 'bondage' trousers from 1977 were also a key part of the McLaren-Westwood unisex Punk look and they spawned countless cheap high-street copies. Look out for the towelling 'bum flap' that makes these an authentic 'Seditionaries' pair. Punk clothes convey a 'thrown together' feel, however hours of hard work went into the design of this 'Boy' T-shirt (above). The zips are YKK (expensive and a mark of good quality) and each one was hand-finished which meant they were never cheap. Beware of bootleg copies made around the same time – some even carry the 'Boy' label, although their fabric is not comparable.

£80-120 (Destroy T-shirt)
£500-600 (Bondage trousers)
£100 (Boy T-shirt)

PLATFORM SHOES

Fashionable seventies footwear carried over the hang-loose 'hippie' look of the late sixties and mixed it with Biba-style nostalgia for the past. 'Platforms' with chunky raised soles and heels once glamorized by Hollywood screen goddesses in the forties, came back into fashion in a myriad of colours and heights that fitted unisex seventies style. Snapped up by men and women, platforms were the only way to show off boot-cut 'flares', which were now so hip. American rock band Kiss, Britain's King of Glam Rock, Gary Glitter, singer Elton John and the Scottish pop sensation, The Bay City Rollers showed just how they should be worn with their outrageous stage versions. These multi-coloured ladies' platform shoes by Emma of London were sheer seventies glamour, made to match glittering disco eyeshadow and tight sequinned tube tops. The price reflects their almost new condition and the fact that they're from a top quality maker. **£500+**

BIBA MAXI DRESS

Pinafore dresses, which had come striding onto the fashion pages late in the sixties – then typically mini – endured well into the seventies. As hemlines fell in this decade, the pinafore no longer oozed that innocent schoolgirl charm, instead it conveyed a practical working gear look – an outfit ideal for the independent woman. Fashion designer Biba tapped into this by turning a printed wool jersey waistcoat into this maxi length pinafore dress. **£100-150**

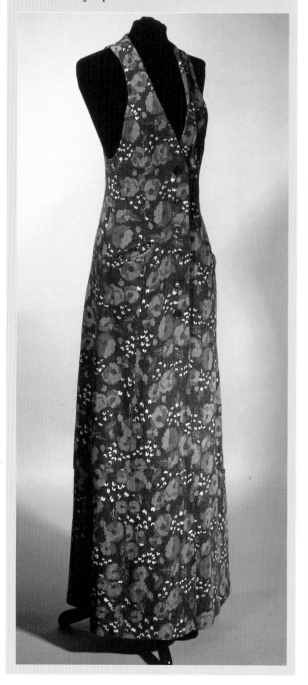

LEATHERETTE COAT

Before the oil crisis of 1973 it was still tempting, reasonably affordable and a real challenge to experiment with plastics. Even though the hippie movement was so vehemently opposed to synthetics. French designer, André Courrèges explored the wet, leatherette look with this coat. The longer length defied his 'pelmet' minis of the sixties and fitted with the dropped hemlines that epitomize this decade. The obvious positioning of the zips above the pockets on the front turns something that's traditionally functional (the zip) into a decorative detail – a trend that became more of a statement when underground Punk fashion was born. Always look for the Courrèges logo, check the security of the plastic poppers and examine the leatherette for wear. Often the plastic coating tears away from the fabric base most notably around the stitched areas and the elbows.
£250-450

DIGITAL WATCH

Credit for the world's first digital watch goes to the R & D team (under John Bergey) at the American Hamilton Watch Company. In 1970 they unveiled a prototype for the futuristic 'Time Computer'; a metal-cased wristwatch with a flashing red LED (light emitting diode) display. To break into the market, examples like this were initially retailed in smart jewellery shops like Tiffany, New York, at a sizeable $2,100 – roughly the same price then as a Chevrolet car! But a new name was needed to stress its revolutionary design. The 'Time Computer' became the 'Pulsar' (after the newly discovered stars) and a legend was born. Today's digital watch revival means quality originals from their heyday are prized. **£600-800**

'FLARES'

A pair of flared jeans was an essential part of seventies dressing. Traditionally classed as men's workwear, jeans had moved on apace and were now accepted fashion classics for both sexes. Paradise Garage in London tapped into demand and became the capital's first shop to sell used denim. At the same time Kelly, Sabrina and Jill (*Charlie's Angels*) wore them in their hit TV series and Barbara Griggs, then fashion editor of the *Daily Mail* said jeans 'add up to instant seventies chic'. This hip-hugging pair with machine-embroidered flowers was made by Stirling Cooper at a time when their new style recruit – British designer and RCA graduate, Antony Price (b.1945) – was turning Stirling Cooper's denim into glam fashion wear. Stiff rivalry amongst jeans manufacturers at the time meant branded buttons and rivets were used – look carefully for little clues. For instance the metal fly buttons on this pair are stamped 'Stirling Cooper'. **£150**

WESTWOOD OUTFIT

The early eighties pop scene championed a historical look – typified by the swash-buckling pirate costume of singer Adam Ant – and trend-setting club groupies cried out for something similar to wear. Self-taught British fashion designer, Vivienne Westwood (b. 1941) was, as always, ready to take fashion in a new direction. She switched from Punk, to become one of the key figures behind the flamboyant, flouncy 'New Romantic' look. This jacket and matching dropped waist skirt from her 'Buffalo' collection (Autumn/ Winter 1982/83), which took its inspiration from the traditional clothes worn by the American Appalachian Indians. On the catwalk, models donned tribal mud for make-up and danced to the sound of folk music. On the street, this style of fashion was readily available. The very distinctive cut of this jacket with full rounded shoulders is a give-away that it's a Westwood product, as is the quality Scottish tweed – one of her favoured materials. But a sewn label inside printed 'McClaren Westwood World's End' is also a clear identification mark. Do check for moth holes in any garments you see – wool is always prone to these if not kept properly. Also make sure that everything is original – that it hasn't been adjusted later to fit or that the simulated tusk buttons have been replaced. **£300-500**

PLIMSOLL SHOES

American designer, Norma Kamali's (b.1945) plimsoll shoes were designed for the glam, shoulder-padded executive woman who wanted something 'casual' like designer labelled jeans to fling on at the weekends. TV viewers were absorbed by the kind of power dressing they saw in long-running soap operas like *Dallas* and *Dynasty*. Shoes like these were an easy way of completing that glossed lipstick and shoulder-padded look. You can just imagine Alexis Carrington (as played by Joan Collins) strutting around in these! The key pointer to Kamali, aside from the label inside, is the way she has cleverly elevated a sports shoe into a fashion item by adding a high-heel. This is a trademark of her dress collections from around this time too. Kamali gained a reputation for taking sweatshirt material and transforming it into desirable business wear. Condition is vital with all shoes and this pair is almost immaculate, which puts a premium on its value. **£600-700**

SWATCH WATCH

The essential fashion accessory for every YUPPIE (Young upwardly mobile professional) – which we all remember as being the buzz word of the decade – was a Swatch watch like this. They first appeared in 1983 and the Swiss manufacturers who made them hoped that their totally novel product would dent the market dominance of big brand Japanese watches – and it did. The Swatch's simple design, with a mere fifty-one components (against ninety-one or more in conventional quartz watches), its precision moulded plastic case, recognized accuracy and an ability to be waterproof to 30 metres made it seriously attractive. But the real carrot for the buyer was its price. First tagged at £23.50, a Swatch was appealingly affordable. As millions world-wide soon discovered it wasn't just a case of owning a watch for life. Styles changed constantly as every year two new collections were created giving wearers a watch to suit almost every occasion. For the hardened fans who wanted to splash out there were special limited editions too, flashed in company as status symbols. Today it's these that are recognised collectables and there's even a Swatch Club who cherish still boxed and unworn examples. Interest is at every level, although the limited edition models (where less than 10,000 are made to commemorate a special occasion) and the select art watches (where an artist or designer styles fewer than 500), are without a doubt the ones to keep. This swatch is one of just 140 styled by French artist Kiki Picasso. Because it was never offered for sale, but presented to internationally-famous personalities, it's a real rarity – hence its value. **£16,500**

'OBSESSION' PERFUME

'Obsession', the fragrance that evoked the sensuality and ardour of an 'impassioned woman', took perfume to unexplored heights when it was launched in 1985. It was the first scent to come from American fashion designer Calvin Klein (b.1942), who shot to fame internationally with his designer jeans, aided by actress Brooke Shields's memorable line, 'You know what comes between me and my Calvins? Nothing!' Obsession's intoxicating blend of floral scents and oriental spices was something entirely new and it unleashed a seductively feminine scent that was as provocative as the advertising campaign to promote it. 'Sensual', 'Powerful' and 'Passionate' were the three words chosen to sum up Klein's new fragrance, aimed at the eighties female executive with hidden romantic fantasies. Interestingly perfume bottle collectors have already put unopened Obsession bottles aside. One reason is that the talented French-born sculptor and perfume bottle master Pierre Dinand (who also styled the packaging for Opium, Ysatis and a host of other fragrances) designed the bottle. An Indian prayer stone in Calvin Klein's personal collection inspired its softly curved outline. Only unopened bottles complete with original packaging will stand the test of time. **£10-15**

'PLAZA' DRESSING TABLE

The ultimate in glitzy bedroom detailing this decade has to be this 'Plaza' dressing table designed by American architect Michael Graves (b. 1934). The bright colours and eclectic Art Deco Classical style are a big clue to the fact that it was a piece for the influential Memphis Group. They made such a big impact on interiors worldwide, believing new design style came from juxtapositioning a spectrum of colours and forms, the like of which had never been seen before. Shocking, fun and exciting, the Memphis-look meant whatever you wanted it to. But the main thing was that it was free from design dogma and took a fresh direction. Inspiration came from fifties and sixties popular culture. The interiors of bars and cafes with their Formica-topped surfaces translated into the whole group's use of laminates. As a collectable it's rather special – the design itself was exhibited at the first ever Memphis Exhibition in Milan (1981) and this version is the 11th 'Plaza' made, which dates it to the early eighties. **£12,000-16,000**

'NEW ROMANTIC' FASHION

Another flowing gem, fitting for the followers of eighties New Romantic fashion. This vivid red cotton smock-style top was styled by the young and gifted British designer, Rachael Auburn, whose baggy outfits were retailed on London's King's Road. Clearly a piece of dress to impress, it's astonishing that there is little sign of wear here. **£100**

HAMNETT T-SHIRT

While it was a decade of high-living and extravagant excesses for some, others were embroiled in protest. And a key focus for the anti-government campaigners was Greenham Common in Berkshire – where the anti-nuclear, anti-missile lobby gathered. Fashion became an obvious vehicle for strongly held opinions, thanks to enterprising British designer, Katharine Hamnett (b. 1948). She printed a range of peace movement T-shirts in silks and cottons with provocative slogans, including the classic '58% Don't Want Pershing', which she wore to greet Prime Minister Margaret Thatcher at a 10 Downing Street cocktail party in 1985. **£30-40**

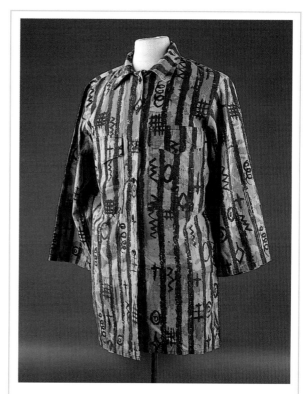

CULTURE CLUB SHIRT

When singer Boy George and his band 'Culture Club' hit number one position in the British pop charts with 'Do you really want to hurt me?' (1982), a new brand of music and an equally new style of dressing was born. Suddenly make-up for men, braided Rastafarian-styled hair and dress-length T-shirts worn over trousers were deemed *de rigueur* costume for the band's young followers. If you shopped in London's trendy King's Road you could get a flavour of the cultural mix that Culture Club promoted. And that was where the band's followers could buy exactly what was worn on stage. This shirt, designed by Sue Clowes, was one of the accessible styles available from the famous 'Review' store. 'It was amazing when you went inside,' says the fan who bought this new, 'They had the whole Culture Club look.' But it was at a price – £35 in the early eighties wasn't cheap. With a revival of interest in the eighties as a whole, it won't be long before fashion like this becomes as sought-after as Dior – so collect while you can! **£50+**

in the bedroom

in the bedroom

JEAN-PAUL GAULTIER PERFUME BOTTLE

From the designer who brought the corset back into fashion ('machinery from another age' as he called it), came this sexy, curvaceous scent bottle, filled with a crisp floral fragrance that carried his name – Jean-Paul Gaultier (launched 1993). At the cutting edge of nineties fashion it's no wonder that the lively French designer (b. 1952) chose such a revealing outline for his perfume – clearly modelled on the bustiers he styled for pop singer Madonna's raunchy 'Blonde Ambition' world tour in 1990. 'My bottle is headless because the perfume is for a woman who represents all women. And I dressed her in a corset, another memory I have of my grandmother. Then I put the whole thing in a tin can because I think cans are beautiful!' explained Gaultier. For a perfume bottle collector, a Gaultier bottle is a *must*. The designer keeps interest astutely strong by constantly issuing new limited run versions to celebrate Valentine's Day and Christmas. Buy one of these now and it could well be a nice little nest egg for the future. **£250+**

WALLPAPER MAGAZINE

A monthly magazine perfectly timed for the nineties. *Wallpaper* (published by Time Inc.), as its name suggests, focuses on 'the stuff that surrounds you' – our interiors, our entertaining style, our architectural environment in context with an element of travel mixed in. *Wallpaper* has become a visual narrative for the super-trendy, devoutly modern readers it attracts. Issues are proudly displayed, coffee-table-style, in offices and homes, keen to convey a sense of upbeat awareness and style. Since its launch issue (September/ October 1996) *Wallpaper* has gone from strength to strength and its status as a bible of nineties style is confirmed. The ultimate is to own this first issue, a treasured copy that few people thought to keep. A complete run of *Wallpaper* from then to now has reputedly sold for as much as £1,000 – a figure that's sure to climb in the future. **£50+**

'ALICE' DRESSING TABLE

British designer Matthew Hilton's 'Alice' dressing table retailed by design specialists, SCP, is more than a purely functional piece of bedroom furniture. It's asymmetrical outline is soothingly sculptural, designed to catch your eye from every perspective – whether you're looking at or looking into it. Like a bird on a perch, the matching stool is a place to sit and preen. A spot where you can lose yourself for a moment and reflect just like young Alice did in Lewis Carroll's adventure *Alice Through the Looking Glass* which gave rise to Hilton's title. An inspired hand-crafted design from a talented furniture maker who's already been picked for the permanent collections of a string of the nation's museums. **£1,500 (dressing table) £260 (stool)**

'COBWEB' DRESS

When you think about nineties fashion you have to look at it's leaders – the Brit pack. Whether it's the supermodel menagerie of Kate Moss, Naomi Campbell and Jodie Kidd or the pioneering Anglophile designers like Stella McCartney and Alexander McQueen who have infiltrated the hallowed world of continential style, this decade is clearly influenced by the British 'cut'. A new contender for the fashion throne and one to watch is the talented Matthew Williamson (b.1971) – a graduate from London's Central St Martin's School. For his first fashion show, he persuaded Kate Moss and Helena Christiansen to take to the catwalk on his behalf. From humble beginnings in the space of a few years his collection is now sold in stores around the world. This 'cobweb' dress from his launch show (February 1997) took its inspiration from nature. 'Like the rest of my designs it bridges the gap between decoration and minimalism, and is perfect for the nineties woman. She wants clean simple silhouettes with flattering details.' Look for the hallmark Matthew Williamson label – an indicator of enduring style. **£700**

PHILIP TREACY HATS

Irish designer, Philip Treacy (b.1967) has reinvented tradition for a modern age. Thanks to his enormous talent and increasingly high profile that's recently seen Treacy win countless awards and step from a successful millinery career into accessories too, the art of hat wearing is now *de rigueur* fashion for the nineties. Youngsters who a decade ago would hardly consider head gear as wearable, boxing hats into fashion for an older generation or a special occasion, now rush to the

High Street to take home a Treacy gem. Because if you look carefully you'll find a range of hats he's been designing for Debenhams diffusion line since 1993. These make a good start for beginners but in years to come it will be his couture range under the 'Philip Treacy Limited' label that will rise high on the collectable scale. Visual statements that are designed to be glamorous and to be noticed, these

hats are as delicate, polished and inspiring as a nouvelle cuisine dish is for the table. Collectors, eat your hat out! Already spotted by London's Victoria and Albert Museum, the Crafts Council (who call Treacy an 'established style leader') and the Hayward Gallery for exhibition, this is a fashion giant who can only get bigger. Make sure anything you buy remains in pristine condition though.
£1000+ (couture) £500+ (ready-to-wear) £120-150 (Debenhams range)

VERSACE

Bright primary colours paying homage to Andy Warhol's screenprinted paintings in the shape of Marilyn Monroe and James Dean portraits, plus the 'Gianni Versace Couture' label, point towards one designer – Italian fashion genius Gianni Versace (1946-97). This is an outfit with a vitality of its own that's intended to attract attention. Think of actress Elizabeth Hurley's headline-grabbing safety-pinned evening gown or that one-shouldered blue dress worn by Diana, Princess of Wales, and you have a sense of the impact the late designer's creations have. Although Versace's first branded womenswear collection appeared back in 1978, there is plenty of reason to start collecting couture pieces from the nineties now. As is the way with collectables, interest has increased in labelled Versace pieces since the designer's death and that's set to continue. You'll find many of the Versace fashion empire's creations (now under the direction of his sister and brother, Donatella and Santo) have already found a home in museum collections around the world. Auction houses like Christie's have started to reflect growing collector interest with sales of Versace originals like this too. **£400-600**

LULU GUINNESS HANDBAGS

Lulu Guinness's (b.1960) handbags have dangled from the wrists of Madonna, Liz Hurley and the Duchess of York not forgetting Patsy Kensit who clutched one when she married Oasis singer, Liam Gallagher. They may be little gems (the emphasis being on 'little' because space inside is limited to 'make-up, money and keys') but Guinness's handbags have gathered a loyal following, since their appearance in 1990. Entirely self-taught, she's re-introduced feminine frivolity to the working woman's wardrobe. 'I want to glamorize and feminize the British woman,' she says. And with bags like her signature 'rose basket', a satin and floral miniature spectacle, who wouldn't feel the focus of attention? A range of limited edition models (in runs of little more than a hundred) like this 'House' handbag appeal to collectors, who already include London's Victoria and Albert Museum. Spotting a Guinness creation, as opposed to a cheap copy, isn't difficult – just think of quality (lashings of hand-embroidery) and attention to detail ('all our bags have matching vanity mirrors'). **£130-425**

FARAH LISTER JEWELLERY

Farah Lister's (b. 1962) dramatic original costume jewellery designs – exquisitely made from the finest materials (often antique gem-cut glass) – are specifically styled to turn heads. This is quite simply 'jewellery to die for' from a gifted designer who's the Coco Channel or Elsa Schiaparelli of the nineties. Collectors already pay thousands for their costume jewellery originals from the thirties and forties so it won't be long before Farah's pieces are held in such high esteem. It's hard to believe such talent was all self-taught but that was how Iranian-born Farah started out a decade ago. Now she's the darling of Britain's catwalk designers and even styles exclusive one-offs for the likes of Bruce Oldfield and Tomasz Starzewski. So what could be nicer than wearing your collectable and looking glamorous at the same time – just look for the distinctive Farah Lister mark on the back and you're made! **£55-2,000 (necklaces) £45-200 (earrings)**

IN THE
Nursery

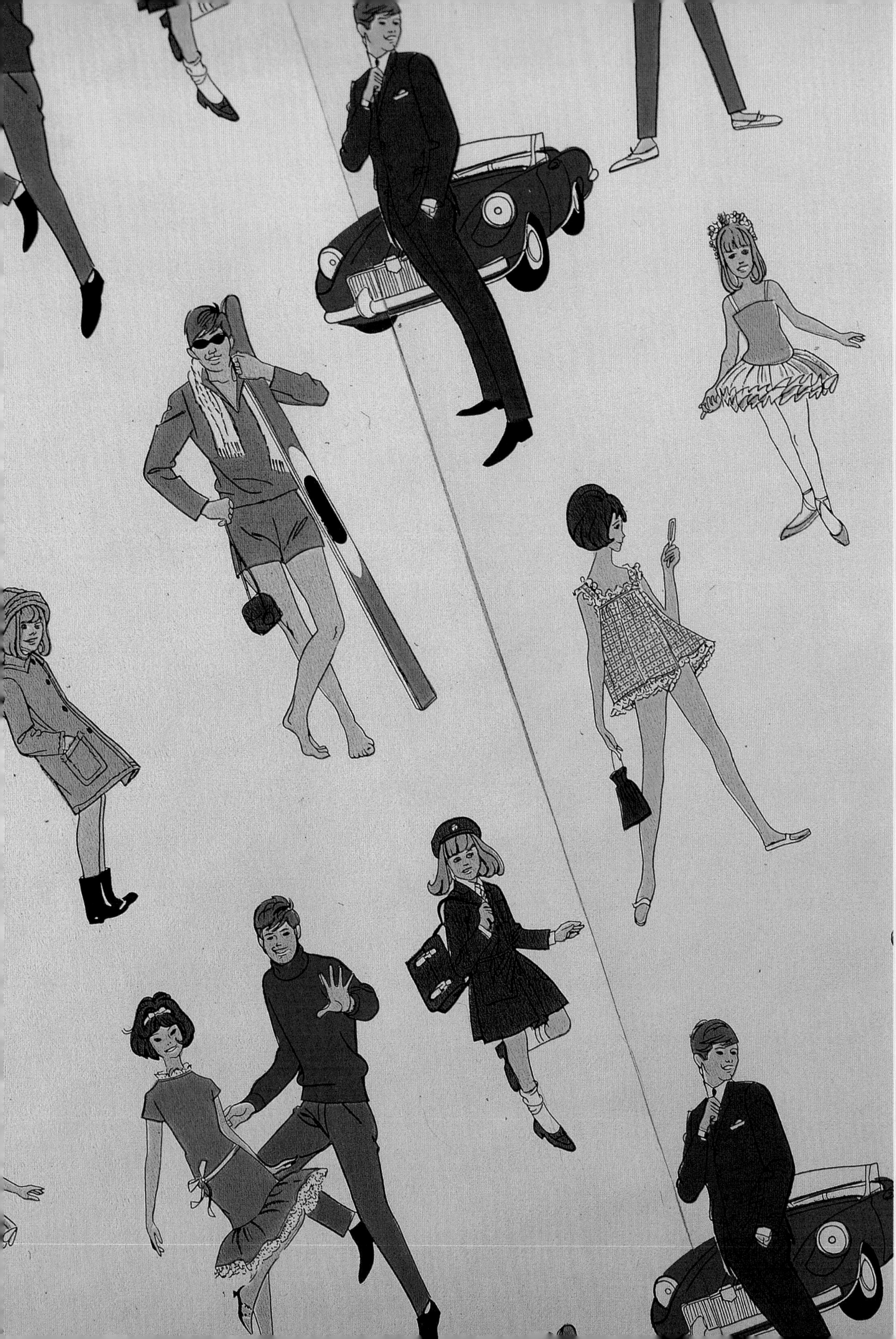

For the post-war baby boomers, growing up was an entirely modern experience. Their parents sought the advice of Dr Benjamin Spock, whose child rearing manual *Baby and Child Care* (published in America in 1946) advised parents to feed their babies when they wanted to eat rather than sticking to a strict schedule. It was a caring, sharing approach that encouraged newly prosperous fifties households to pamper their children by buying them the latest playthings.

By the fifties, Britain's toy factories were back on civilian track after production had been diverted to aid the war effort a decade earlier. In the course of making core parts for military equipment, the toy makers had learnt a great deal. Hard plastic, for instance, was the perfect material for dolls heads and bodies. This coupled with new injection moulding techniques meant dolls could be easily and quickly mass marketed. The spin-off from mass production was of course, price, and toy makers pounced on demand for pocket money toys by selling in individual boxes rather than traditional sets.

For girls and boys starved of new toys throughout the war years, advances like this were a blessing. Rival firms like Pedigree, Palitoy, Rosebud and Todd & Co Ltd. (Roddy) claimed their dolls' were the 'most beautiful' and 'most realistic' despite their similarities. Boys were more preoccupied with robots (after the sci-fi classic, *Forbidden Planet*) and motor transport. Britain's first post-war motor show in 1948 unveiled a new line of cars that gradually filtered through to the streets. Meccano Ltd, who made Dinky Toys, resorted to reissuing pre-war models in fashionable fifties colours in order to meet demand. Gradually the diecast industry caught up and popular new lines like Lesney's Matchbox toys and Mettoy's Corgi toys appeared. When it came to the launch of the Triumph Herald in 1959, a miniature version was released simultaneously.

As consumerism started to boom, radio and television became a more familiar form of home entertainment for children too. The BBC launched *Listen With Mother* in January 1950 and Andy Pandy made his first appearance on screen in July of the same year. Toy makers were quick to pick up on youngster's enthusiasm and broadcasting's new stars – Muffin the Mule, Sooty and Sweep and Noddy –were all made as toys, and popped up in countless books and annuals.

Towards the end of the decade further advances in the plastics industry brought vinyl into the nursery and one of the first dolls to champion the new material was 'Barbie' in 1959. With her feminine curves, pouting red lips and stilettos, Barbie appealed to young girls who looked forward to being part of the new 'teenage' generation.

Although the Space Age officially began in the fifties, it was the sixties that saw the most significant progress. This was the decade that closed with the whole family gathered round their television set to witness man's first steps on the Moon. So it's no wonder that schoolboys cried out for realistic rather than fantasy models to re-enact those historic moments. Like a growing proportion of sixties toys, these were Japanese imports skilfully made from a mixture of tinplate and plastic for the Western market.

Long-running sci-fi series like *Dr Who*, *Thunderbirds* and *Star Trek* spawned an array of official and unofficial merchandising that was snapped up. One of the most sought after toys of the decade was James Bond's Aston Martin DB5. In the run up to Christmas 1965 there was a 14-week waiting list.

By the seventies the glory days of diecast and tinplate were over. Nursery toys were largely made with plastic parts and the established British firms faced pressure from cheap Chinese imports. Industry statistics said that traditional playthings no longer appealed to 12-15 year olds as they'd done in the fifties – now the average upper age for toys was 11.

In the eighties, most children's energy was expended in the brainpower needed to solve the newly marketed Rubik's cube. But parents didn't have to spend money to entertain their young ones. If you bought a Happy Meal from fast food giant, McDonald's then you received a plaything for free. Nineties American toy giant, TY Inc also aimed their Beanie Baby toys at children who love collecting.

The unpredictability of a toy's life keeps everyone on their toes and ensures there's plenty of demand. Condition is a vital factor that affects all toys today. Of course some clever youngsters are already ahead of the game and their bedrooms are filled with autographed memorabilia from popular nineties' bands. Whether it stands the test of time remains to be seen.

WADE POTTERY'S 'WHIMSIES'

When the Wade pottery (est. 1810) unveiled its miniature animal figures, better known as 'Whimsies' (for their whimsical look), they were an instant hit with the public. Sir George Wade, the man behind their launch at the British Industries Fair in 1954, came up with the idea of 'pocket money toys' priced at 5s 9d per set. Needless to say their brightly printed boxes and limited runs caught on with adults too. Ten sets of aptly named 'First Whimsies' (most with five models in each), appeared between 1954 and 1961. This is the last – Set No. 10 (Farm Animals) the rarest and most valuable of the run because of its short production span (1959-61). It's also the set whose figures are most commonly faked (look out for horses that won't stand up and poorly modelled swans, because the Shire Horse alone can fetch as much as £125!) Two points to remember, 'Whimsies' from the fifties are not all marked because there was little room on some for the Wade stamp. Don't confuse these early runs with Wade's individually boxed and numbered 'English Whimsies', which found their way into most homes in the seventies, eighties and even nineties (in the case of re-issues). Although these were also pocket-money toys or even Christmas cracker, tea packet and crisp freebies, they're still not in the same league and don't appear in Christie's auctions yet. Prices for common 'English Whimsies' in mint condition hover at around £2-5 each, although rarities can be worth more especially if they're still boxed. **£300+ (Set 10)**

ENID BLYTON'S NODDY

Lovable, adventurous Noddy and his entourage of friends first appeared in Enid Blyton's *Noddy Goes To Toyland,* which was published in 1949. The little fellow who brightened up millions of youngsters' lives with his everyday tales in a fantasy world was Britain's answer to Disney's Mickey Mouse. Noddy spawned every collectable imaginable – annuals, puppets (after his show made for ATV) and even board games. First editions of the Noddy stories, illustrated by Dutch artist Harmsen Van Der Beek (d. 1953), are avidly sought after now. There's similar interest in tinplate toys like this. Made by British wholesaler, Morris & Stone under their 'Morestone' label, this is one of a series of Noddy cars they made (here, Noddy is cast in lead). It may be a little bashed around the edges but few of these toys have survived with their boxes from the fifties. **£140-180**

HARD PLASTIC DOLLS

During the war years, doll firms used their resources to develop plastic components for the aircraft industry. Therefore it was only natural that plastic was the material that they opted for after peace was declared. Driven by the parents of the post-war 'baby boomers', who demanded new quality playthings for their little darlings, the hard plastic doll was born. For the first time dolls were light, unbreakable and remarkably realistic, with 'combable' rooted nylon hair, fluttering eyelashes and a cry that would make you weep. Butterick's, McCall's and Simplicity printed endless patterns for home-sew dresses to keep dolls' wardrobes fashionable. Besides the classic baby and little girl dolls, Princess Elizabeth was reproduced in hard plastic to mark her Coronation by Lines Brothers Ltd (est. 1919) under their Pedigree tradename. She was promoted as 'Elizabeth – the dressmaking doll' and *Woman* magazine's fashion designer Veronica Scott styled a range of patterns for stitch-yourself Elizabeth outfits. By 1956 the heyday of hard plastic was over as flexible, softer vinyl took its place. Nostalgia is the driving force behind most collectors, who have learnt to avoid 'put-togethers' with mis-matched body parts. Fortunately the key makers (Pedigree, Rosebud, Roddy and Palitoy) nearly always left their mark – look for it between the shoulders or on the back of a doll's neck. **£80-150**

BEATRIX POTTER'S MRS. RABBIT

Fifties bedtime stories were almost certain to include Beatrix Potter's tales. To make them even more memorable, British firm Beswick (founded 1894), joined forces with Potter's publishers and copyright holders, Frederick Warne & Co, to launch a range of 'Beatrix Potter's delightful characters in pottery' (from 1947). 'Mrs. Rabbit' who appeared in 1950 carrying her basket filled with 'a loaf of bread and five currant buns', joined a run that already included her husband Peter and Benjamin Bunny. Well-known characters like these were popular and are still made now (although modern versions have brown marks rather than the early gilt mark). However, it's the figures that didn't appeal that fetch astonishing prices today. Potter's *The Pie and The Patty Pan* story was great fun to read but Beswick's model of Duchess (the dog) carrying a bunch of flowers, was so black that you couldn't make out her features. Compared to the others, her run was relatively short (1954-67) and that means she's like gold-dust today – worth an astonishing £1,500-2,000, providing there are no chips at all! **£100-150**

Surrounded by older brothers and sisters, who were rocking and rolling to the new fifties sounds, baby sister wanted her own teenage role model to worship. Firms like Pedigree and Roddy ran a line of vinyl 'teen dolls' in the late fifties, who, despite their 'high-fashion clothes' and ponytail hair, still had a baby-face look. However, that all changed when Ruth and Elliot Handler, who ran American toy company Mattel (est. 1945), launched Barbie in March 1959 (although she didn't reach Britain until 1961). Promoted with sentimental TV advertising, Barbie was the fashionable doll who was 'really real' with feminine curves, alluring 'doe-eyes', glamorous outfits and pointy high-heels, which made her an unrivalled success at a mere $3. Dolls from the fifties and sixties are prized, as are today's limited edition and collectors' Barbie dolls. This is a rare early Barbie from 1959, dressed in her *Roman Holiday* ensemble, capturing actress Audrey Hepburn's chic, after the 1953 film of the same name. It's worth remembering that for a matter of months in 1959 Barbie came on a pronged stand – these very first dolls have locating holes in their feet and are the most valuable today. Successive improvements like bendable legs (1965) and turn 'n' twist waists (1967) help with dating. The outfits provide a good clue, because they were the height of fashion in their day, so they're fairly easy to date. Original boxes add to Barbie's overall value and the most sought-after items of clothing have to be her stilettos – so many pairs fell off you're lucky to find a doll that still has hers. Do watch out for poor quality fakes with newly drilled locating holes. **£1,000+**

'CHEEKY' BEAR

Teddy bears were given a boost after the war with the birth of Brumas, London Zoo's cuddly-looking polar bear cub. However, the traditionally hand-made variety now faced stiff competition from cheap, machine-stitched Far Eastern imports. Old established firms like J. K Farnell (est. 1840) – who made the teddy that inspired A. A. Milne's 'Pooh' in the twenties – were forced to look at new conveniently 'washable' and less expensive synthetic fabrics and stuffing. To speed up production some firms even imported automatic stuffing machines from America. At the same time English makers Merrythought (est. 1930) introduced a totally new-look teddy in 1957. Their 'Cheeky' bear, as it was known, was a loveable big-eared character with bells in its ears, a pinched nose and an over-sized head. This 'Cheeky' is fitted with glass eyes, but as the decade closed, ultra-safe, orange plastic lock-in eyes (a safety feature invented in 1948) replaced them. Early versions were made from traditional golden mohair or silk plush, but by the sixties nylon plush was more common. Look out for the Merrythought label stitched to the bear's right foot.
£150-250

In the fifties tinplate robots went hand in hand with pulp fiction novels, 3D B-movies, the sinister overtones of the Cold War, a peculiar fascination for flying saucers and not forgetting the invention of far smaller batteries, which made the whole robot explosion possible. Post-war Japan flooded the market with toys that no child could resist – especially after the release of the sci-fi movie classic *Forbidden Planet* (1956). It introduced the super-human 'Robbie-the-Robot' and spawned countless licensed and unlicensed 'Robbie' toys. When you're talking about real robot rarities, look no further than this 'Lavender Robot' (a non-stop model) made by Japanese toy giant Masudaya (est. 1724). It's one of the famous 'Gang of Five' – a quintet of robots made for American kids from the same tinplate shell (1956-59). With its primitive lithographed rivets it doesn't look desperately advanced (although 'Radion', another in the series, did work by remote control) and this is the sort of toy that today's nostalgic collectors long to own, even with the rust spots and scratches. Nearly all were played with and most were replaced when something better came along. Boxes do exist, but they are so rare that they are not worthwhile waiting for. However, you can still be lucky – for example, this robot was recently found in a car boot sale where it changed hands for £1 before being sold at Christie's for far more.
£800-1,200

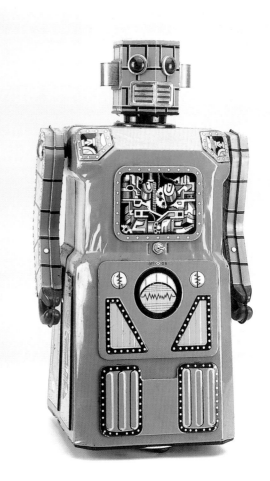

DAN DARE'S RADIO STATION

Comics were still staple reading for schoolboys, but the Superheroes of the forties were losing ground to far more sinister horror stories by the time the fifties arrived. Parents were dismayed and moralists frowned, believing that cartoon strips were leading their innocent youngsters astray. In America a Comics Code with strict content guidelines was introduced, while in Britain, Parliament pushed through a 'Horror Comics Bill' to ban US imports. Dan Dare was the upstanding and quintessentially English hero who stepped into the breach. Branded 'The Pilot of the Future' he appeared in the pages of the new *Eagle* comic from the day it was launched in 1950. Although he was purely fictional, schoolboys acted out Dan Dare's 'Save the Universe' adventures with the help of toys like this radio station made by Hertfordshire-based toy firm J & L Randall Ltd under their 'Merit' label. The collectability of this example lies in it still being boxed and complete half a century after it was made.
£100-150

TEENAGE BOOK

While advertisers were trying to get to grips with the buying patterns of the NEWLY BRANDED 'Teenage' generation, tailor-made reading like this *Teen Age Book* told independent youngsters what their mothers didn't! Inside its glamour-girl cover young girls had all their questions answered – 'What Shall I Wear?' was followed up by five informative pages of fashion tips, Constance Spry gave cookery advice and screen idol actor James Mason was sprinkled throughout to prolong the attention span! **£15**

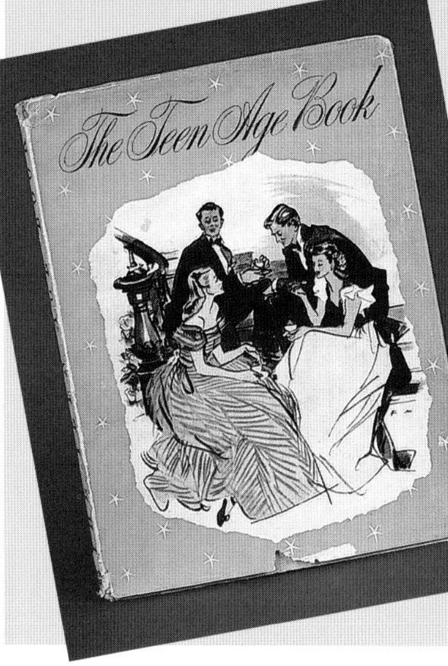

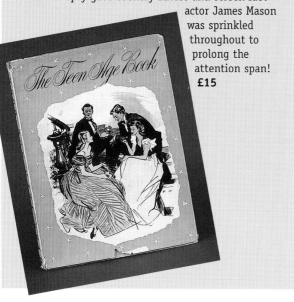

MUFFIN SWEET TIN

Along with Andy Pandy and Sooty, Muffin the Mule was a star of BBC children's television. Sunday wasn't Sunday for boys and girls without the clip-clopping of Muffin's hooves and the sing-along lyrics of his co-star Annette Mills. He was operated and designed by Ann Hogarth whose deft actions brought the jointed string puppet to life, to the extent that children wanted their own versions of Muffin at home. Consequently a variety of Muffin merchandise, like this Huntley and Palmer's sweet tin, appeared in the shops. **£15-20**

DINKY TOYS

Starved of toys during the war, youngsters were eager to catch up when toy firms like Meccano Limited (1901-79) got back into action. The fifties and early sixties were the heyday of their diecasts, which first appeared under the famous 'Dinky Toys' label in 1934. As post-war prosperity and optimism gradually filtered through to Britain's homes, cars like the Morris Oxford, launched at the 1948 Motor Show, became regulars on the road. And what better reminder of a young boy's outings to the country with his parents than a pocket-money version of the real thing? Always keen to show they could move with the times, Meccano also changed the way Dinkys were marketed and even set up a Dinky Toys Club to capitalize on youngsters' interest. Instead of simply selling gift sets and single toys from trade boxes as they'd done before the war, they broadened their appeal by packaging their toys in attractive individual boxes as well. Today these boxes sometimes prove more valuable than the actual toy! The numbering system printed on the side helps with dating, because by 1955 the traditional number and letter combination had been replaced by a sequence using numbers only (eg the 40G became Dinky model no. 159). Similarly, 1958 saw Dinky models appear with realistic glazed windows. Their 'Supertoy' range of larger vehicles (launched in 1947) also kept them way ahead of the competition. Of these, it's the advertising lorries that collectors drool over today. This Heinz Big Bedford (1955-58) is like gold dust if it appears with a ketchup bottle instead of the tin of baked beans shown here and it's twice as desirable if, like this one, it has survived unblemished with its original box. **£250-350+**

'MATCHBOX' TOYS

Making diecast toys so small that they could fit into a matchbox-sized box was a clever idea that originated from British toy makers Lesney (founded 1947). Their 'Matchbox' toys – marketed by a distribution company called Moko – undercut Dinky toys with their 1s 6d price tag when they first appeared in the toyshops in Coronation Year (1953). This meant children could afford to buy one toy a week and collect the entire series without too much saving up. The scale was a little erratic, with saloon cars appearing the same size as a London bus like this (from 1957). But millions of children warmed to their miniature appeal and knew where they were with their collecting thanks to the clear numbering system on both the model and the box. Because of that, these pocket-sized treasures were known as the 1-75 series. Good condition early models, all quality pieces with hallmark metal wheels, are rapidly climbing in value.

£15-30 (depending on condition)

C.S. LEWIS BOOKS

When C.S. Lewis's book, *The Lion, the Witch and the Wardrobe* was published in 1950, a true fantasy world for children was born. Reading styles changed and children's literature moved into a new realm as the mythical style of storytelling replaced traditional schoolboy and girl adventures. Flick through the pages of this copy of Lewis's final Narnia story, *The Last Battle* (which first appeared in 1956), and you can see how illustrator Pauline Baynes brought the magical Kingdom of Narnia and all its curious creatures to life. First edition copies of this title and others in the series are rapidly climbing in value providing they are presentable without any torn pages, scribbles or Sellotape! Dustjackets – which most of these books were issued with – add considerably to the overall value. For example, *The Lion, the Witch and the Wardrobe* could sell for close to £2,000 in its original paper cover! **£950+ (*The Last Battle* – first edition with slightly damaged dustjacket, a pristine copy would be worth more)**

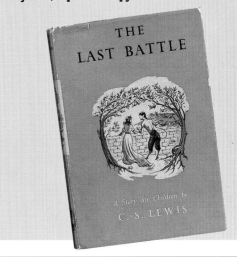

FOOTBALL SCRAPBOOK

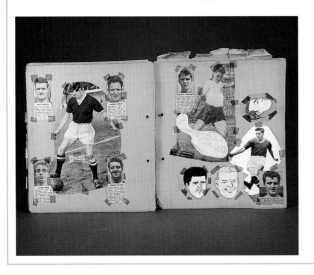

Football boomed after the war as fans, desperate to return to the entertainment they knew and loved, tuned their televisions in and packed the nation's stadiums. For a father and his son it was a fun day out and even better if they could catch a glimpse of the talented Manchester United team, 'The Busby Babes'. A *Manchester Evening News* reporter had coined the phrase after Busby had fielded 21-year-old Roger Byrne and 18-year old Jackie Blanchflower in 1951. By 1956, the Babes' average age was just 22 and they astonished the public in 1957 by winning the League Championship again and reaching both the final of the FA Cup and the semi-final of the European Championships. No wonder countless schoolboys kept a scrapbook like this, charting their heroes' progress, tragically curtailed by the Munich Air Crash (6 February 1958), which killed eight of United's players. **£500-1,000**

SINDY AND PAUL

Sindy, 'the doll you love to dress' was Britain's upbeat answer to Barbie. When she made her TV debut in 1963, she wore this snazzy 'Weekenders' outfit ('for casual parties'), one of several really modern creations designed by Carnaby Street's hip team, Foale & Tuffin (whose revolutionary sixties clothes were regularly modelled by Twiggy). Pedigree, the firm who first made Sindy (she's now made by Hasbro Inc.), told retailers to get 'with it' and wise up to the doll who promised to be 'the new rage'. Catchy jingles on her record, 'Dolly Beats' and on her launch TV commercial were enough to persuade plenty of girls that Sindy was the doll to own. Jigsaws, annuals, a phenomenal wardrobe of over 150 outfits plus her own regular magazine page (*Sindy's Scene*) and a Club (Sindy's Club) helped to reinforce her personality and seal her success. With her is boyfriend Paul (named after the Beatle, Paul McCartney) who joined Sindy as a doll in 1965. The roll of Sindy wallpaper seen at the beginning of this chapter (page 83) dates from 1966 and amazingly it's never been used. You can see Sindy posing in her 'glamorous pink and white check baby-doll' nightdress, her bell-bottom blue jeans from Weekenders and her 'out-of-this-world' sparkling Dream Date dress. As Barbie prices spiral upwards, doll collectors are turning their attention to pristine, still boxed Sindy originals like these. **£100-140 (1963 Sindy) £40+ (1965 Paul) £20-30 (Sindy wallpaper)**

CORGI'S 'CHITTY CHITTY BANG BANG'

The 1968 big-budget movie *Chitty Chitty Bang Bang* 'the most fantasmagorical film ever made', was based on a children's adventure story that few prople realize was written by Bond author, Ian Fleming (1964/5). Its undisputed star, alongside Dick van Dyke (as Caractacus Potts) and Sally Ann Howes (as Truly Scrumptious), was 'Chitty', the magic car 'that can travel on land, on sea and in the air'. Corgi Toys, scaled down 'Chitty' was just as exciting for the children who received it for Christmas that year. When you flipped the handbrake forward out popped red and orange striped wings and separate stabilizer wings clipped front and back 'to steady her flight' in

the air. This may be one of the most memorable toys of the decade but against Bond's Aston, it was an expensive plaything at 22s 6d and far fewer were sold. Because most were played with, it's models like this, still in their original 'illustrated window pack', complete with all four figures, that are fought over. **£150-250 (mint and boxed)**

SASHA DOLL

Swiss artist Sasha Morgenthaler (1893-1975) came up with the very distinctive sculpted features of the 'Sasha doll' to try and make a plaything that would have a broad appeal to children, whatever their race. This reflected the more open attitude of the sixties and a growing need for toys for a multi-cultural society. The British firm Frido (who became Trendon Ltd in 1970), were licensed to make Sasha dolls commercially (from 1965) alongside German makers Gotz-Puppenfabrik (from 1964). Helped by improved vinyl techniques they achieved a look that was universally popular by varying the tint of the doll's skin to suit its hair colour. Needless to say, Sasha dolls were popular, but they were also expensive, so far fewer were made than of the multi-million-selling Barbie. All Sasha dolls (including brother 'Gregor' and the 12 inch long baby) were sold with a circular wrist tag saying 'Sasha' on their right hand. To help today's collectors the highly sought-after German dolls are marked on their back and necks with the Sasha logo but, apart from looks, Britain's Frido/Trendon dolls have no helpful hints at all. **£100-160**

ACTION MAN

It's incredible to think that over 30 million Action Man dolls have been sold to date and it all started here, when American toy giant Hasbro (est. 1923) – who'd been so successful with GI Joe in the States (from 1964) – licensed the British toy firm Palitoy (est. 1919), to make the same 'moveable, fighting' dolls for the UK market. It was only after extensive research that Action Man made it to Britain in 1966. After all, boys didn't and wouldn't play with dolls said the trade in the sixties and GI Joe's military name could never be a recipe for success in Britain where anti-Vietnam War feeling washed across the Atlantic. But Palitoy persisted and commissioned sample surveys, which revealed that boys really did enjoy getting a fighting doll dressed, ready for action. The firm's group sales director, Harry Trowell, came up with a new name that 'reflected his all–round action pursuits' – and the aptly branded 'Action Man' was born. This 'Action Soldier' is one of the three launch figures (the others being 'Action Pilot' and 'Action Sailor'). If you examine an early doll like this closely you'll notice that metal pins are used to make the moveable joints while later models have plastic joints instead. All the figures carry the same GI Joe-style battle scar on the face but the moulded, cropped hair and hard plastic hands are give-aways that you're looking at an early figure. Fuzzy spray on hair didn't arrive until 1970 – two years after the pull-cord voice box let Action Man talk, and soft plastic grip hands were a later feature too. It wasn't just Action Man that every boy had to own, it was the hundreds of accessories – life rafts, a tiny pencil that really wrote and even a storm lamp that worked. Rare sets that are still wrapped can fetch more than the dolls themselves. Because prices for both have rocketed so much, beware of mix 'n' match figures – ones where the various body parts didn't start out life together.
£120-200 (boxed, with original outfit)

MINIC ROUTEMASTER

The classic double decker of the sixties was the AEC Routemaster, one of the last buses to have the hop-on, hop-off platform at the back and the engine at the front. Such a familiar feature on the road as it replaced all the old trolleybuses, it's no wonder that every boy wanted to own a model like this made by British firm, Tri-ang Toys (est. 1919 as part of Lines Bros). It's one of their famous 'Minic' models, a successful range of 'push and go' clockwork models made from tinplate which rivalled dinky diecasts. You needed to save 14 shillings to buy it new but you did get a superbly detailed scale model right down to the promotional slogan, 'Routemaster – Try out your new London bus' on the side. Widespread nostalgia drives most bus collectors and the Routemaster era is a favourite. Condition is everything and this model is virtually A1, even the tyres that so often perished look almost new. **£400-500**

1966 WORLD CUP

Britain's greatest sporting moment in this decade was England's World Cup football win on home ground on 30 July 1966. Millions saw the England v Germany match screened live on television, while fans lucky enough to get tickets for the final converged on the Empire Stadium, Wembley, to share the joys and the tears of the players at first hand. It was a tense time as Germany's No 6, Wolfgang Weber, scored an equalizing goal in the dying seconds of the game. That forced the match into extra time where West Ham player Geoff Hurst took England to a 4-2 victory with two winning goals. Around a million of these official souvenir programmes were printed and as you can imagine, most have been kept – hence their relatively low value now. **£30**

NASA SPACE STATION

When NASA's (National Aeronautical Space Agency) Apollo II crew landed on the Moon in 1969 the whole world watched with bated breath. Space had been a preoccupation throughout the fifties but a decade later, with televised pictures reinforcing the reality of galactic travel, toys needed to be well made and believable. So although a truly fictional product, this tinplate NASA space station made by leading Japanese toymaker, Horikawa (est. 1959) was designed to be as technically accurate as possible. The doughnut shape, to create artificial gravity, resembles the docking station in Kubrick's space fantasy *2001: A Space Odyssey*. Five windows gave you an almost realistic insight into everyday space life (or how it might be) with views of the dining area, communications, rest and recreation, the command room and the engines. Strangely collectors don't swoop on ultra believable models like these, they prefer fifties fantasy robots. So it's a good time to collect. Blue is relatively common, red is more unusual and tends to carry a higher price tag. **£250-350**

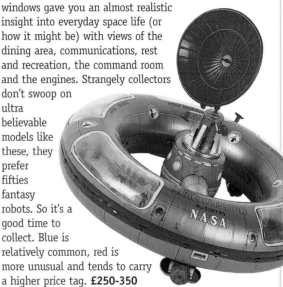

JAMES BOND

When the first James Bond movie, *Dr No* (1963), brought Fleming's British secret agent 007 to life, every schoolboy dreamed of being Sean Connery. Therefore it's not surprising that a host of official and unofficial merchandising pandered to their yearnings. Probably the best known of all because close to 4 million were sold is the Mettoy Company's (est.1936) model of Bond's gold Aston Martin DB5 from *Goldfinger*, sold under their well known Corgi Toys trademark. Its launch in 1965, a year after the release of the film, was perfectly timed for Christmas. However, the run on toy stores meant that demand outstripped supply. The *Sun* newspaper reported that Mettoy were 'sending out convoys of 35-foot trailers from their Swansea factory, all loaded with tiny, gold-painted Aston Martins.' Yet there was still a fourteen week waiting list for the 9s 1d car with 'retractable machine-guns and over-riders for ramming villains', a bullet-proof screen that popped up from the boot to 'deflect shots from pursuing counter-spies', and an ejector seat. Mint and boxed is the key to a true valuable here, as there are plenty battered versions around. It's also worth keeping an eye out for the far rarer remodelled silver version with revolving number plates and red nylon tyre slashers from 1968 – worth far more. **£100-200 (mint and boxed)**

THUNDERBIRDS

After Russian cosmonaut Yuri Gagarin became the first man to explore space in 1961, the lines between what was fact and fiction quickly blurred. Without a doubt that contributed to the success of TV series like *Thunderbirds,* which was aired in Britain from 1964. Even though the puppetry was blatantly obvious, youngsters found the plot bewitchingly real. For instance, International Rescue's founder, Jeff Tracy, had been an astronaut himself and in the storyline was one of the first men to walk on the moon. Series creators Gerry and Sylvia Anderson (the voice of aristocratic Lady Penelope Creighton-Ward) took the Thunderbirds' string puppets into the year 2026 with truly futuristic vehicles. One of the most memorable was Lady Penelope's FAB 1 – a six-wheeled pink car, styled on a Rolls Royce with a natty way of parking (each wheel rotated so it could manoeuvre into a space sideways). This toy version of the FAB 1 made by Dinky Toys appeared in 1966, complete with figures of Lady Penelope and her driver and dedicated servant, Aloysius 'Nosy' Parker! Sadly the box is damaged, which does reduce its value but it still has all four plastic rockets and the 'flying spur' mascot on the top of the radiator, which is often broken. Look out for the sought-after luminous pink version too. And if you happen to come across a Thunderbirds' puppet from the series – prepare yourself for a shock. An original Parker recently sold for £19,550 and Sylvia Anderson's own Lady Penelope marionette made an astonishing £34,500.

£80-100 (in this condition, up to £350 in mint)

FLINTSTONES

Hannah-Barbera studios' lovable tale of the prehistoric Flintstone family was the first prime-time cartoon series made for television. And although it premiered from 1960-66 in America, countless repeats across the world and blockbuster films have sealed its legendary success. Even now every minute of every day someone, somewhere tunes into *The Flintstones.* So it's not surprising to find a whole series of licensed (and unlicensed) Flintstone collectables – early licensed bits are hot property today. This is Fred's battery operated 'Flivver' (his car) from the sixties, which mixes lithographed tinplate with plastic. It's made by American giant the Louis Marx Toy Company (1921-80) who kept their prices for quality toys tantalizingly low by setting up a manufacturing plant in

Japan. Original boxed condition (ie the unplayed-with look) is a real bonus here. And there's more interest in battery operated toys because they're generally better quality. You can't fault this toy because it's been shop stock all its life, which explains its pristine condition. **£300-400**

SPACEHOPPERS

We remember them so fondly, but where are all those Spacehoppers now? Promoted as 'the amazing inflatable riding ball' Spacehoppers (distributed by the Mettoy Company) were a feature of most homes because they were not just teenage toys, but ideal for adults too! With the help of a bicycle pump you could inflate the brightly coloured vinyl playball to suit either you or your children (although the standard orange 'Trend Spacehopper' was recommended for young ones). 'Try having a competition with your friends to see who can jump the furthest and the highest' said the instructions! They remained popular well into the seventies and are still made today, although collectors (and there are some) look for sixties originals. It's unusual to see a surviving box but this one doesn't match this orange Spacehopper – on the front you can see pictures of the rarer blue version. Because most were left too near a radiator inside or were punctured outside, period originals are proving hard to find. **£28**

PIPPA DOLL

With her long centre-parted hair, Pippa from British toy makers, Palitoy was a real seventies girl. But unlike other vinyl dolls from this decade she took a new direction in the form of her easy to carry pocket-size – a mere 6½ inches (17cm) tall. So girls could happily take Pippa and quite a few of her look-alike friends (French 'Marie', pale 'Tammie', suntanned 'Britt' and 'Emma') to school in a specially designed case printed with her name. Pippa was stylish (she lived in a flat-pack seventies house full of Danish designed furniture), she was fashionable (there was a Boutique playset complete with Pippa's outfits) and most of all she was affordable, you didn't have to choose just one doll, you could own the whole range. Many youngsters were tempted to cut Pippa's silky hair and most played with her rather than kept her boxed like this. **£15-30**

RAYMOND BRIGGS

It was a gamble for British author and illustrator, Raymond Briggs (b. 1934) to take one of the world's best-loved characters, Father Christmas, strip him of his sentimentality and turn in him into one of us. But when his first book, aptly titled *Father Christmas* was published in 1973 it received a warm welcome and won Briggs the Kate Greenaway Award that year for his illustrations. This was humour at its subtle best. Father Christmas experienced everyday human problems and it was funny to see him grumpy because his home in the North Pole was so cold or because he was too plump to squeeze down a chimney. In his pictures, interspersed with a few of Santa's words, Briggs anticipated every child's concerns and added a new element of realism to youngsters' tales. First edition copies of this and his books that followed like *Fungus the Bogeyman* (1977) and *The Snowman* (1978) are shooting up in value.

£75-80 (*Father Christmas*, 1973)
£35-40 (*Fungus the Bogeyman*, 1977)
£45 (*The Snowman*, 1978)

'MR. MEN'

The 'Mr. Men' characters created by Roger Hargreaves (1935-88) have been such a part of growing up since their beginnings in 1971 that it's hard to believe there's a booming interest in first editions of every story. 'Mr. Tickle' started it all with his unfeasibly long arms, which could reach out and tickle people or stretch down to the kitchen to prepare his own breakfast in bed. Soon a whole series of other characters followed, 'Mr. Greedy', 'Mr. Happy' and so on, with well over 40 to date. This is a copy of the first *Mr. Men Annual*, which was issued just before Christmas 1979. Because the series was aimed at the very young, most first edition copies of the stories have torn pages, scribbled covers and are generally very tatty. Look carefully at the condition before you buy. **£25**

BAY CITY ROLLERS

The tartan-clad Scottish pop group The Bay City Rollers were every teenage girl's dream, when they appeared on TV's *Top of The Pops* singing their first number one hit 'Bye Bye Baby' (1975). This was sing-along music with a refrain that was so simple you couldn't help but hum it wherever you went. Sexy lead singer Leslie McKeowan was every young girl's hearthrob so what better way to show you loved his voice and the band's music than wearing these iron-on jean badges? There was an official *Bay City Rollers* magazine, a thriving fan club and the group even had their own TV show, *Shang-A-Lang*, to boost their popularity. This jigsaw is another of the many mementoes from their heyday (if you can bear it, always check they're complete). By 1979 the band had changed their name to the 'Rollers' and their hit days were over.

£3-5 (patches) £5 (jigsaw)

STAR WARS

In 1977, the multi-million box office hit *Star Wars* took space adventure into a new ultra-realistic realm with a fast action storyline and fantastic special effects. It was the first of the *Star Wars* trilogy, written and directed by George Lucas and needless to say it spawned a host of merchandising from cereal packets, to posters and toys. Although they

were treated as car boot cast-offs a decade ago, with the recent digitally enhanced re-release of the *Star Wars* films, officially licensed pieces (courtesy of Lucasfilm Ltd) are now fought over by collectors. Kenner (part of American toy giant Hasbro) made the bulk of the 3 ¾ inch scale toys (based on Luke Skywalker being 5 ft 10 in). These revolutionized the toy soldier world because they were made from plastic but instead of being rigid were fully movable. Something to remember is that they were widely promoted and over 250 million of these action figures sold, meaning they're not all hugely valuable. Large action figures like this 'fearsome interplanetary bounty hunter', Boba Fett, from *The Empire Strikes Back* (1980), are sought after because they had a limited run. This 13-inch figure was launched well before the film to promote the fact that a new character was coming. Always check that figures like these are complete – rocket tips and 'Wookie scalps' have a habit of getting lost! As a tip, loose Star Wars figures tend to be worth less than those still packaged, unless they're real rarities like one of the elusive pre-production Boba Fetts with a spring-loaded rocket firing backpack – valued at over £1000 today. It was never sold because the firing mechanism didn't work.

£80-120 (13-inch Boba Fett)

MAGIC ROUNDABOUT

It only had a five minute slot before the early evening news on the BBC but *The Magic Roundabout*, created and narrated (from 1965) by actress Emma Thompson's father, Eric, was extremely popular. Over eight million children regularly tuned in to see Dougal the shaggy dog who only ate sugar, Dylan the rabbit, Ermintrude the flowery

pink pink cow, Florence, Brian the snail and Zebedee, a strange spring-loaded character! The BBC licensed various firms to make Magic Roundabout memorabilia, from cloth books to bubble bath, and in 1971 British firm Corgi was allowed to make toys. This Magic Roundabout playground, which cost £6.30 when it was first sold in 1972, was their best. When you wound the blue plastic handle the track turned and moved the train, it also rotated the carousel. The show's memorable theme music played as Dylan rotated too. Fabulous condition toys like this still in their original boxes are rare. **£300-400**

STYLOPHONE

Described as 'the greatest little instrument of the century', the Stylophone was a firm children's favourite in the seventies. London-based firm, Dubreq Ltd., who came up with this best-seller ensured their 'pocket electronic organ' would be an instant success by making it easy to play, cheap to buy and by getting well-known children's entertainer, Rolf Harris, to promote it. All you needed was a simple numbered teaching book, included in your boxed package, and a Rolf Harris record to make sure you got the sound right, then hey presto – you were an electronic musician! Collectors today tend to be cult Stylophone fans who nostalgically remember touching that metal 'keyboard' with what looked like a biro (the stylus). They've tracked down three different colour variants so far (black, white and woodgrain) but, apart from that, the standard Stylophones are very similar – all came with an 'organ' on/off switch, optional vibrato, single

speaker and one stylus. Complete boxed versions like this are in demand. Also look out for the rarer deluxe model – the 350S – 'many instruments rolled into one'. It was aimed at the truly dedicated Stylophone player. Powered by a pair of 9V batteries, it had two styluses, presets and other advanced features like an input for a footpedal and external audio input for running the sound of a 'tape, record player or rhythm unit' through the integrated speaker. All in all, it was 'a virtual pocket orchestra'.
£25 (standard boxed model)

CHOPPER BIKE

'Once there were ships. Then there were aircraft. Now there is the Hovercraft … and the wild new fun bike from Raleigh'. Alan Oakley (b. 1927) was the British designer at the forefront of the famous 'Chopper' bicycle. Launched in 1970 in two colours, red and yellow, it took its name from the American term for helicopter and gave kids the sort of street 'cred' and independence they'd been waiting for. At a launch price of £32 it was a third more expensive than a standard children's bicycle. But when it was the ride most youngsters aged six to twelve had dreamed of, who cared? Oakley looked to the style of the American high-rise bikes for inspiration although the Chopper he styled for British bicycle firm, Raleigh (est. 1887) was a new breed of pedal-power altogether. This precious Mark 2 version distinguished by a sloping main tube and curved back tube appeared in 1971/2 – a development of the launch model with a straight cross bar. The 'Arrow Wedge' branding was adopted to identify this new-look tubular steel frame, which tied the Chopper's classic large back wheel and smaller front one together. A high-back seat gave kids a 'rocking chair ride' and the spectrum of strong colours – anything from amber (based on a pint of Worthington's beer) to red, purple and in this case, silver – made friends who didn't own a Chopper jealous. But by the mid-seventies, the market was saturated and interest in Chopper bikes started to dwindle. Those who kept their originals were clever because renewed interest, conventions and now a Chopper club have put the King of the 'wheelies' back on the map again. **£300-500 (in pristine original condition)**

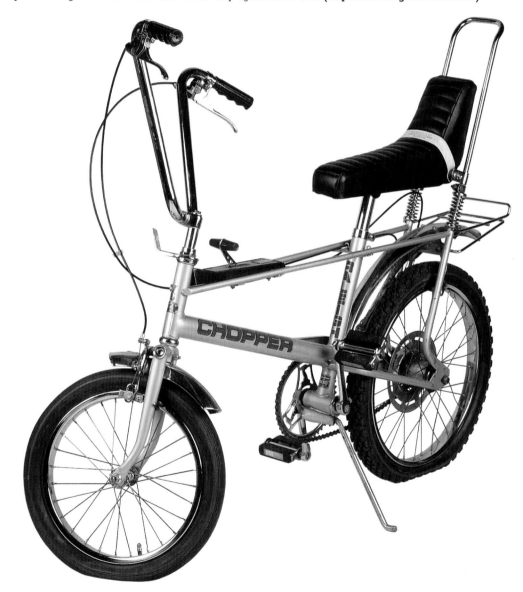

CABBAGE PATCH KIDS

In 1983 Cabbage Patch Kids® became all the rage after they were officially launched in toyshops around the world. Children couldn't get enough of the soft dolls. Although they were made in their thousands, they retained their own identity with individual names and a birth certificate to prove it. They were 'born' in 1976 when an American student, Xavier Roberts sold home-stitched fabric dolls called 'Little People' at local craft fairs. As interest grew, clever Roberts came up with the idea of adoption. He gave each doll a name, taken from a thirties baby book, and told 'parents' the charge was a homing fee. Then BabyLand General Hospital opened in the States where the 'Little People', still largely hand-made, were delivered by nurses and doctors from a giant cabbage patch. Media interest spurred on demand and in 1983 American toy giant Coleco (est. 1932) was licensed to make the first mass-market dolls. They were slightly smaller than Roberts's 'Little People' and were branded 'Cabbage Patch Kids'. These dolls are still made today (by Mattel) but at the moment it's those Coleco issues that collectors seek. As a clue to dating look for the trademark 'birthmark' (Xavier Roberts's coloured signature on the doll's bottom). Each year the colour changed starting with black in 1983 then green (1984), blue (1985), red (1986) and so on. This 'haute-coiffure' doll was made for cabbage patch lovers in France. **£15-20+**

NATWEST PIGS

When Britain's NatWest Bank wanted to give youngsters an incentive to save, they approached the great Wade pottery to design a series of moneyboxes. In 1983 the famous NatWest pig family was launched. As a child's nest-egg grew so did their Piggy family, beginning with Woody (for investors with £50) and ending with Sir Nathaniel (given to those who managed to save £500). The offer ran until 1988 and thousands were made but relatively few children managed to complete the set – £500 was a large sum for a junior saver then.
£250 (for all five pigs)

ROALD DAHL BOOKS

Collectors eagerly snap up first editions of all the books by the great children's author, Roald Dahl (1916-90). Although he wrote for youngsters in the sixties, starting with *James and the Giant Peach* (published in 1961 in the USA, 1967 in Britain), it's his adventure tales from the eighties that brought him international acclaim. One of the best-known is the story of the *BFG* (1982) with Quentin Blake's (b. 1932) classic illustrations, which is already climbing in value. The charm lies in the storyline, a 'big friendly giant' who catches dreams and blows them into children's rooms that is just as appealing to adults as it is to younger readers. In *Revolting Rhymes* published a year later, Dahl keeps everyone on their toes by taking six well-known and loved fairy tales and re-telling them with a humorous twist. First edition copies are well worth seeking out providing they still have their dust jackets. One of the more unusual copies to watch for is *Dirty Beasts*, which was initially illustrated by Rosemary Fawcett (1983). In 1984 it was re-issued with Quentin Blake's drawings. Collectors will pay a premium for the former, even though the text is the same.

£40-50 (*BFG*, 1982) £40-50 (*Revolting Rhymes*, 1982) £45-50 (*Dirty Beasts* – Rosemary Fawcett illustrations) £35-40 (*Dirty Beasts* – Quentin Blake illustrations) £35-40 (*The Witches*)

FAME ANNUAL

During the eighties, the BBC screened a weekly series considered essential teenage viewing – *Fame*. First a blockbuster movie starring Irene Cara (1980), it was aired as a TV series (in the USA from 1982-3) and trailed the ups and downs of life in New York's High School of Performing Arts. Its fictional characters, the disruptive Leroy Johnson, drama queen Doris Schwartz and unlucky in love keyboard player Danny Amatullo, were so familiar to most youngsters they were almost part of the family! So an annual like this was a welcome present. For those tempted to collect and re-live their youth, check the condition of any annual before buying. Many youngsters completed the puzzles, tore out the pictures and wrote in their names, which detracts from the value. **£3**

MCDONALD'S™ HAPPY MEAL TOYS

Premiums or give-aways have long been a clever form of securing brand loyalty for products, but when fast food giant, McDonald's™ issued their first freebie plastic toys (1970s in the USA, 1985 throughout the UK) little did they realize what a phenomenal collectable they would spawn. The aim was to use these well made toys to promote their Happy

Meals™ for children but as new runs appeared and old sets became fought-over, they proved equally appealing to adults too. Specialist collecting groups, books and magazines have evolved solely devoted to these and other fast-food collectables so it's no wonder that rare sets have changed hands for hundreds of pounds. It's important to remember that, on the whole, to make a set worthwhile keeping, it must be complete. That means the correct Happy Meal™ box or bag, a full complement of toys (they can run to eight in Europe, as many as 21 in the States) and, if appropriate, all the insert cards. This Fast Macs series was the first UK McDonald's™ promotion.
£15-30+ (depending on the figure)

MODELS OF YESTERYEAR

Models of Yesteryear date back to 1956 when they were first made by Lesney Toys (est. 1947). By the eighties, the model cars that had delighted youngsters for generations were also catching the eyes of their parents and Lesney responded by presenting an ever-extending range of road classics in attractive boxes with cellophane windows. Eager collectors young and old kept these largely plastic models as potential nest-egg material. But sadly this is one category that hasn't made any millionaires yet. So many were sold that prices are still very low although a few of the rarer models are appearing grouped together in auctions. **£2-20 (depending upon model and condition)**

BOY GEORGE

To his fans who adored him, Boy George (born George O' Dowd), lead singer of the cult band 'Culture Club' was just as the slogan on this box describes, 'The original outrageous boy of rock'. This 'fully poseable doll' made by American firm LJN in 1984, is now a sought-after collectable in its original packaging. Those who remember it as 'the toy of their generation' with its long 'stylable' hair are eager to re-acquire pristine packaged models. And with the current revival of interest in the band and recent new and re-released singles, this is a toy that's set to rise in value. **£100-30**

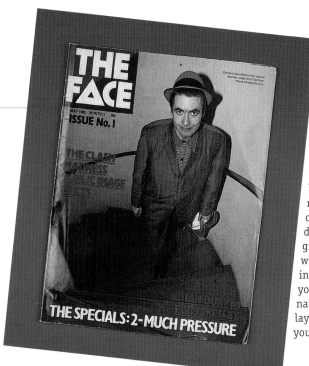

One of the most influential style magazines of the decade was *The Face*, and this is Issue No 1, published in May 1980. A 60p bible of street fashion, it was branded 'the kid's shiniest codebook' – unmissable reading for restless teenagers keen to carve out their own identity. Owner and editor, Nick Logan, was the driving force behind the magazine with memorable graphics from the talented Neville Brody (b.1957), which culminated in the 'Magazine of the Year' award in 1983. *The Face* was overwhelmingly influential in the youth market and high-street fashion stores and national banks were quick to borrow elements from its layout and graphics for their brochures to lure trendy youngsters their way. **£10-20**

BOYZONE

Like many of the hottest pop bands in this decade, it was a newspaper advertisement that brought Britain's BoyZone together. It was placed by the owners of a Dublin night-club who, in 1993, were looking for an all boy group to perform live on stage. With subsequent hits like 'Love Me For a Reason' and 'All That I Need', they've rivalled and outlasted Take That to become one of the most memorable pop sounds of the nineties. So these limited edition 'BoyZone dolls' by British maker Vivid Imaginations are set to be future treasures. Each member of the Irish quintet (Mike, Keith, Ronan, Steve and Shane) is realistically represented in vinyl and the presentation box includes an 'exclusive autographed poster' – actually carrying a facsimile signature but still a nice extra that you should remember to keep.

£50-80 (mint and boxed set)

SPICE GIRLS

The 'Spice Girls' are a nineties pop sensation whose 'Girl Power' music and merchandising has reached almost every home, just as the mass of Beatles' memorabilia did in the sixties. They started as a gang of five, Mel B (Scary Spice), Mel C (Sporty Spice), Emma (Baby Spice), Victoria (Posh Spice) and Geri (Ginger Spice), who shot to international fame after their debut single 'Wannabe' reached number one in the UK charts in July 1996. That started a record-breaking run of six consecutive number one hits in the space of just eighteen months plus a movie, *Spice World*, which turned the five girls, who again had responded to an advertisement, into pop super stars. Astute young collectors of officially licensed Spice Girls merchandise are buying two bits at a time – one to play with, one to keep. But because of the quantity produced it's likely to be the more personal mementoes that escalate in value. The owner of this Spice Girls promotional postcard was careful to get it signed by each band member. Because it includes Geri's signature (before she left the group in May 1998) it's already a valuable record of the band's beginnings.

£200-300

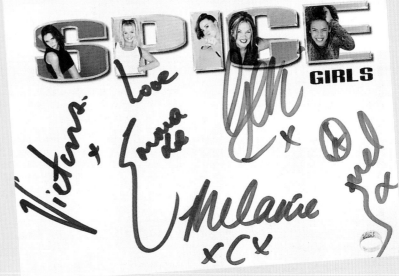

COLLECTORS' STEIFFS

For teddy bear collectors (or arctophiles as they're officially known) the name Steiff is still the buzzword even after a century of production. The German firm, named after its inspired founder Margarete Steiff is credited with giving us the world's first jointed plush bear in 1903. Even now the limited edition collectors' bears they make, like this replica of a 1908 Steiff teddy, are as finely made as the originals were. The plush fabric or fur is made from mohair and instead of cheap plastic this bear has glass eyes. Although teddies should be played with, collectors' editions (this bear is one of only 3,000 made) are strictly for the shelf only.
£100

BEANIE BABIES

American toymaker, Ty Inc.© has tailored its phenomenally successful 'Beanie Baby' line for children who love to collect. These well made bean bag toys, which first appeared across the Atlantic in 1993, are now a multi-million dollar business. Unpredictable runs, rapid 'retirements' (when a toy is no longer sold) and constant new issues keep children and now adult collectors on their toes. So far over 200 different Beanie Babies are known and collectors vie for the real rarities like the dark blue elephant – an accidental colour run which lasted for barely a month in June 1995. At a guess there's only about 2,000 of these around and the once cheap $5 toy has reputedly changed hands for over $3,500. Would-be hoarders must keep the cardboard 'swing tags' attached and in pristine condition. Specially made plastic tag cases are vital if you want to prevent creases reducing the toy's value. As well as being a mark of a genuine Ty toy (that's important as there are plenty of bean bag imitators) these tags are a good guide to dating. One to look for is the first generation tag (1993-94), a full red Ty heart (now it's clipped on the left). This was attached to the nine original soft toys. Because most of these were removed and thrown away, they're now collectable in their own right! This is a first edition 'Britannia' beanie bear, 'born' 15 December 1997 (the model made in Ty's Indonesian rather than Chinese factory). Because it's a Ty UK Ltd, exclusive, American collectors who are unable to buy this toy back home are desperate. They will pay handsomely to add 'Britannia' to their collection.
£100-300 (depending on condition and origin)

RCP2 CHAIR

Take a mass of polyethylene shampoo and conditioner bottles, mix in the odd few milk cartons, a plastic coffee cup or two, some old Marks & Spencer coat hangers and a few used yoghurt pots and hey presto – you've got a chair for your child's bedroom! British designer, Jane Atfield (b.1964) was one of the first to consider recycling waste plastic in Britain after she found herself paying a fortune to import it for her furniture designs. Using old plywood presses from the thirties she compresses what was once our rubbish into sheets of multi-coloured plastic. 'The process is quite simple,' she says, 'All you need is heat and pressure. And by using this old machinery, it's rather like we're recycling the machines too.' The Victoria and Albert Museum and the Design Museum have already snapped up an example of her best-selling RCP2 chair for show. This smaller child's version is made from offcuts of the larger adult chair. 'The material is quite expressive,' she says, 'children recognise what it is immediately.' For the future this is certainly a piece you won't be able to forget.

£95 (for child's chair – £150 for the adult version)

OASIS

Pop band autographs are always worth collecting especially when they're from the cult nineties group, Oasis (formed in 1991). The Gallagher brothers (Noel and Liam) have been branded 'The new Establishment' after Noel accepted an invitation to meet Prime Minister Tony Blair at No 10 Downing Street. They've certainly come a long way since April 1994 when they scraped in at No. 31 in the charts with their single debut 'Supersonic'. Their first album, 'Definitely Maybe' released later that year shot straight to No. 1 and became the fastest-selling debut album ever with over 3.6 million copies sold so far. With a fan base that matches the Beatles on an international scale, Oasis are classed as ambassadors of 'Cool Britannia' and this black and white publicity photograph, signed by all five band members is already a collectable with potential. **£300-400**

SONY

oasis

PHOTO CREDIT: JAY STRAUSS

POP-UP BOOKS

Pop-up books have been with us for over a century thanks to a run of inventive Victorian publishers. But modern day production techniques have replaced the once rudimentary fixings and hand cut shapes so pop-ups can now be far more complex. The idea of a book with moving parts that once only appealed to a very young age group has been snapped up by nineties publishers like Dorling Kindersley (est. 1974) who make a range of pop-up and self-assembly paper models as study aids for older children. Inevitably they're opened, assembled and enjoyed but some clever collectors are keeping their copies in mint, unread condition. With interest in children's books already soaring you'll be glad you kept these first editions fifty years from now. **£10-15**

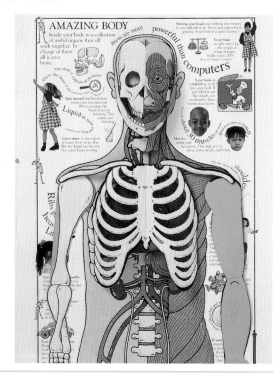

FOOTBALL MEMORABILIA

Football memorabilia is one of the fastest-growing collecting areas and Sotheby's matched the surge of interest with their first ever Football Auction in 1998. Although a string of club shops have opened in cities around the country selling a range of team souvenirs, these mass-market items are not destined for great things in the future, simply because so many are sold. Fans who want to make sure they have a real collectable to keep would be wise to make their visit to a home game twice as rewarding by waiting to get their programme or even a shirt like this autographed. Because the 1997 England squad (including BBC Sports Personality of the Year, 1998, Michael Owen) added their signatures to this shop-bought replica shirt, it's become a cherished item. **£100+**

IN THE
Study

in the study

Sinclair

ZX Spectrum

CHESS

The study was traditionally the male domain. For those households lucky enough to have one in the fifties, it was a place to unwind away from the hubbub of the family. Home working was a concept that just didn't exist in civilian life. The only time men were seen in the house during the day was at lunchtime when over half of Britain's factory workers returned home for their midday meal. So the study was generally used in the evenings and at weekends. After a hard day in the office helping Britain's industries get back on their feet, a man could catch up with the latest news on the Spy scandal or read one of his new James Bond novels, shut away in his own space.

But Daddy wasn't isolated from the latest design schemes. Like every other room in the house, the study was influenced by modern fifties style right down to the atomic 'ball' clock on the wall. It was important to convey modernity at home to the boss who was invited for dinner and that meant having new office-style furniture. Charles and Ray Eames's moulded fibreglass chairs were a statement of affluence, but they were also an expression of contemporary style. If they failed to impress, then the new Leica M3 camera was sure to seal a promotion. Aimed at accomplished photographers, but also bought by wealthy amateurs, the M3 was a boy's toy that became the world's most famous camera.

The study became more adaptable during the sixties. New household gadgets were gradually eroding the notion of an exclusively male space. For instance, as the travel industry boomed and holidays abroad became more of a reality than a fantasy, taking snaps or buying tourist views on coloured slides was commonplace. Many a child who grew up in that decade will remember their father setting up a projector and screen for the whole family in the confines of his study.

Again, modern design had a part to play in the styling of office equipment that also found a place in the home. Italian designers were at the forefront of thinking that aimed to make objects like typewriters less elitist. Olivetti's all-in-one 'Valentine' model was made from the high street's most fashionable material, moulded ABS plastic, and was coloured bright red to fit into every sixties house.

However, the greatest innovation that filtered through to the study was transistorised microelectronic technology, which launched the information age. Although it was pioneered in the fifties, by the sixties it was really harnessed for everyday equipment, including the study's favourite desk accessory – the memorable warbling Trimphone.

When the American Apple Computer Company unveiled their groundbreaking Apple II in 1977, it ignited the personal computer revolution. Now any sort of information could be held on computer: words, charts and data. Few homes were lucky enough to have such a gem but it spawned a series of more affordable machines that brought the family firmly into Dad's domain.

In the eighties cheap home computers also made great games machines. Graphics and sound meant youngsters could simulate the thrill of arcade games in the comfort of their own home. Often it meant using the TV as a screen, but gradually they encroached on the study. The breakdown of the study into a family space was underlined by the new Special Range of telephones launched by a liberalised Post Office Telecommunications Division, which meant that the study desk was decorated with Mickey Mouse who cleverly doubled as a handset and base.

Like every other room in the house, the nineties study is all about style. The gadgets and accessories are not only effective they also look good, being produced from the latest materials. So whether it's the humble calculator that's been given a make-over by Alessi or the desk phone that's been turned into a digital dream by Swatch, striking design and versatility are the keys. Home working has come full circle and is now a viable option for mothers who want to maintain a career. The barriers of fifty years ago have finally been broken down and now you're likely to find Mum working in the nineties study and Dad in the kitchen.

in the study

EAMES CHAIRS

American designer Charles Eames (1907-78) was credited by the *Washington Post* as 'the man who changed the way the twentieth century sat down'. It was chairs like this that brought Charles and his business partner/wife Ray (1916-88) into the spotlight. Taking advantage of manufacturing advances and surplus wartime materials, the Eames' presented excitingly new, affordable designs that didn't rely on timber – which was in short supply at the time. For example, the distinctive body-hugging shell of these chairs came from moulding a single sheet of fibreglass-reinforced plastic (a technique used in WWII to make aircraft radar domes). For versatility, the seat could be attached to a variety of spidery metal bases. Needless to say, Eames furniture was quick to catch on in offices and homes after advertising stressed that it was 'lively, colourful and fun to own'. This chair is a mass-produced version of their 'RAR' (a rocker) made by the American Herman Miller Company. It was an expensive business importing these into Britain, but after Hille Ltd of London began to manufacture the Eames' designs

under licence, a piece like this seemed more realistic to own. Stores like Heal's became a showcase for the Eames' work but the £15 price tag on this chair (equivalent to an average week's wages) meant it was still an expensive luxury for most people. Look for either moulded marks or labels underneath, which point to the Miller or Hille connection. As you might expect most of these ended up in offices and many have been destroyed, hence their collectability today. **£500 (RAR chair)**

Charles and Ray Eames' 'Lounger Chair' and 'Ottoman' was popular back in 1956 when it was first issued. However, interest in the Eames – thanks to a recent retrospective exhibition of their work – has refuelled enthusiasm for their designs and a duo like this is now much sought after. In an era when America was full of optimism and gadgets – the 'Lounger' fitted in. Its slick rosewood-veneered plywood frame was moulded to make it supremely comfortable, whilst silky-soft leather cushions meant this was another 'must-have' for the home. The story of its design goes back to Billy Wilder, the film director and a friend of the designers, who wanted something to nap on in his office – hence the 'Lounger' was born. Telling the vintage collectable apart from modern issues is a matter of examining for wear and tear and looking closely at the labels. **£1,000-1,500 (with ottoman)**

LEICA M3 CAMERA

The launch of the Leica M3 rangefinder camera in 1954 was a groundbreaking moment for accomplished photographers. Those lucky enough to own one (they cost nearly six months' salary) cherished this finely crafted 35mm camera, which became the benchmark for optical focusing. Often referred to as 'the world's most famous camera', it was yet another gem from the German optics manufacturers Leitz (est. 1869) who gave us the world's first commercially successful 35mm camera (the Leica I) back in 1925. To make life easy, the M3 dispensed with time-consuming screw lenses and replaced them with easy to change, bayonet-mounts with an adapter for Leica devotees so their old lenses fitted on the new M3 body. With features like a viewfinder system, which, for the first time, worked with lenses of different focal lengths, plus its lever-wind film advance (instead of the old winding knob) this was the camera to own. Other M3 gems included a hinged back that flipped open for easy film loading and an extremely quiet shutter. Precise serial numbering and thorough factory records means every version is traceable and that's part of the thrill for serious Leica collectors. The crème de la crème are M3s from the first batch, numbers 700,000-700,800 (1954) – the better the condition, the higher the value. **£600-800**

FESTIVAL OF BRITAIN GUIDE

The Festival of Britain (1951) was about 'fun, fantasy and colour' according to its director-general, Gerald Barry. It was also a moment for 'national reassessment', a display 'of the nation's ingenuity' and importantly an opportunity for Britain to celebrate the dawn of a modern age. So, when the South Bank's turnstiles opened on 3 May 1951, the site proved to be more of a draw than anyone had anticipated. Bright colours and exciting new shapes were set against a backdrop of awe-inspiring futuristic architecture – like the towering 300 foot 'Skylon', (winner of the competition for the best vertical feature). Clad in shiny aluminium, it looked just like a rocket, fresh from the pages of the *Eagle* comic. Over 8.5 million visitors in the space of five months flocked to see the mesmerizing array of stands – even though most of the goods on show were hardly a buyable option for a country still restricted by rationing. This was a place to forget that and look ahead. Modern homes for modern living was the theme of the *Homes and Gardens* pavilion and visitors experienced the wonders of life, the universe and everything in 'The Dome of Discovery' (itself the world's largest, spanning 365 feet). The whole Festival experience was a complete contrast to the wartime years of 'make do and mend'. Visitors came away 'feeling alive' and huge numbers returned time after time. As you can imagine countless souvenirs were made and plenty still survive. This is a deluxe copy of the South Bank exhibition catalogue, probably leather-bound to mark the opening day.
£40 (exhibition guide deluxe edition)
£10-12 (normal soft-backed exhibition guide)

BALL CLOCK

In a decade that saw the opening of the first nuclear power station (harnessing atomic energy for electricity), the atom was the fifties symbol for progress and style. It appeared on everything from curtains to pot stands, even finding its way into the study. Although American architect-designer George Nelson (1908-86) came up with the idea of this 'ball clock' for the Howard Miller Clock Company in 1949, its styling was immensely influential throughout the fifties. Twelve birch balls mark the hours radiating from the centre on brass spokes – a fashionable design for 'the Atomic Age'. Look for the 'Howard Miller' stamp and if possible the original winding key. **£400**

ERICOFON

The 'Ericofon' (known as the 'Cobra' telephone because of its snake-like stance) was an icon of the fifties, starring in countless movies of the decade. Ralph Lysell and Hugo Blomberg, the Swedish team who designed it, subscribed to the belief that if you've got malleable plastic, then why not use it. So, together with makers L.M. Ericsson (founded 1876) they styled the world's first all-in-one telephone, with a dial in the base of the handset (the push button Ericofon 700 came in 1976). Sculptural moulding made it a pleasure to hold whether you were left- or right-handed and it was practical too, with a disconnect/connect button on the bottom so it automatically answered when you picked it up. However, cramming the contents of a base and a handset into one unit meant that the Ericofon was heavy and its bulk obscured the caller's vision. In Britain, these stylistic flaws weren't an issue – we could only dream of design like this. The Ericofon was not an option for a nation required (until the late seventies) to rent two-piece hard-wired units from the GPO. Brightly coloured Ericofons were introduced in the mid-fifties with aqua, pink, white, chartreuse and light blue being the earliest. Check the plastic body for cracks and scratches. **£85**

Casino Royale (1953) by British author, Ian Fleming (1908-64), was the first novel to introduce the now legendary British secret agent 007, James Bond. Published at the height of the Cold War, it appeared just two years after the Burgess/Maclean spy scandal rocked the nation. *Casino Royale* was almost certain to be a thrilling success, because the exploits of the suave Mr Bond seemed far closer to fact than fiction! Fleming went on to write another thirteen Bond stories, which inspired the phenomenally successful series of Bond movies that followed (from 1962). Hardback editions of his books from British publishers Jonathan Cape are prized, with a first edition copy of *Casino Royale* like this with its original dust-jacket (styled by Fleming himself) classed as the ultimate. They're a rarity now because the majority of the 4,750 copies were so well-read that their paper covers have either disappeared altogether or survived in a very tatty condition. First editions of Cape's other Bond novels like *Live and Let Die* seem to be hardier survivors and consequently don't command such high prices. Later editions, book club editions and paperbacks (issued in far greater numbers) are more common, so they're correspondingly cheaper. **£1,000-2,000 (*Casino Royale,* first edition (1953) with dust-jacket) £250 or less (without dust-jacket) £150-250 (*Live and Let Die,* 1954)**

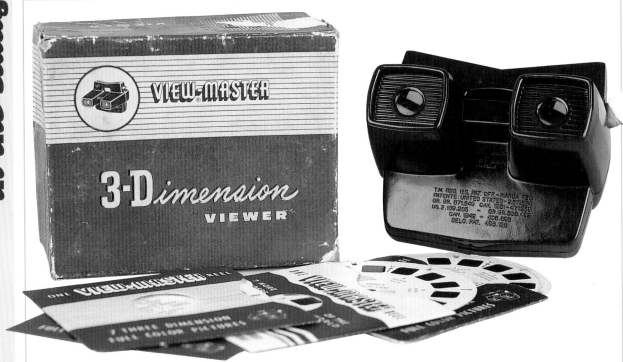

VIEW-MASTER

Although we think of View-Masters as being children's toys, in the fifties they were just as popular with adults. When you look at the reels themselves – featuring anything from views of National Parks to Roy Rogers – it's hardly surprising they were so captivating. In America (where the View-Master made its debut in 1939), cinemas had large versions in their lobbies to promote forthcoming Hollywood features. The idea of a stereoscopic viewer wasn't new when American inventor William Gruber and Sawyer's Inc. (who marketed the View-Master) came up with theirs although they did improve on it. Instead of just one scene per card (like traditional stereoscopes) they offered seven realistic views using Kodak's new Kodachrome colour film. When Sawyer's started making View-Masters in Belgium in the fifties the European market boomed. This streamlined model E was their new lighter, easy to handle version available from 1956. It's styled in the most common colour, 'décor brown' Bakelite with an ivory Bakelite lever. Look out for the rarer red, grey, cream and maroon viewers – they were only ever made in Belgium.
£16 (Model E View-Master) £2 ('European Views' reels)

PIRALI TABLE FAN

Even the most basic fifties gadgets like table fans were treated to a dose of distinctive design. Gone were the days when function dictated form in a dull monotonous way. This fan was styled in Italy by engineer Ezio Pirali (b.1921) who became the Managing Director of Zerowatt, the Italian firm that manufactured it. It powered its way into the future, like a rocket in flight, with its motor and rubber blades suspended from a chromed wire cage. No wonder this desk accessory was chosen out of 5,700 other new Italian designs to be one of just a handful of products to receive the coveted Compasso d'Oro design award in its inaugural year, 1954.
£1,000

HOME/OFFICE DESK

This home/office desk from the early fifties was all about keeping things tidy! A house that was well organised with plenty of storage space 'has a profound effect on the housewife's problem of keeping the place in order,' stated its designer, American George Nelson (1908-86), in his book *Tomorrow's House*. His solution, as design director of Herman Miller, the firm that made the desk, was to provide good-looking structures that were supremely practical. The top of the desk was left clear for a typewriter, a stack of pull-out drawers on the right kept bits and pieces hidden away and a perforated metal drawer on the left – accessible from the side – meant that files were within easy reach when you were seated. If you weren't happy with its position, the desk's light frame was easy to pick up and move wheelbarrow-style thanks to its castors. A great piece of design from an acknowledged master. **£1,000-1,500**

the Sixties

SISPEN DESK

This desk by furniture makers Sispen was driven by contemporary needs. Homes and offices needed furniture that was easily mass-produced but still offered quality and flexibility. Its basic table structure used a minimum of components and the adaptability came from the drawer cube – a bolt-on attachment that could be placed either side to suit the office layout. To complete the look it was finished in a modern grey, cream and orange paint scheme! A typical example of the era, this would have fitted in very nicely with some of the flat-pack furniture available from Terence Conran's all-new 'Habitat' shop, which opened in London's Fulham Road in 1964. **£450-550**

TRIMPHONE

Remember these? For the British public, the appropriately named 'Trimphone' (because of its slim line) meant liberation when it appeared in 1965. Up until then, the General Post Office (then in control of telecommunications) had offered no choice – it was the standard 700 type or nothing! But now there was this 'new luxury telephone' whose styling was 'the result of a completely original design created in consultation with the Council of Industrial Design'. The Trimphone was a two-tone innovation that responded to modern home-style needs. It was light, infinitely mobile with a new coiled line cord that seemed to stretch for miles, a handset that ran lengthways along the telephone and 'an iridescent dial for immediate location'. Then there was that unforgettable ring, 'a tone caller that produces an intermittent warbling note', which spawned endless impersonations. Despite all those features the high-style Trimphone was passé by the eighties, after a liberalization policy by the newly formed British Telecom (from 1981) opened the floodgates to more modern designs. Trimphones were out and those gathering dust en masse were rapidly recycled to recover the radioactive tritium that had helped their dials glow in the dark. Survivors are now back in vogue, led by the original two-tone colours (grey and white, light and dark blue, and grey and green). There'll always be a lingering fondness for that ring. Watch out for re-sprayed versions in far from original colours. **£50**

SLIDE PROJECTOR

Italian brothers and architects, Achille and Pier Giacomo Castiglioni combined forces to design this 'Rocket' slide projector for Italian lens specialist, Ferrania in 1960. Combining the slide projector's name with the popular fascination for space was a clever way of stressing its cutting edge technology and design. Knowing it's been styled by the Castiglioni brothers, masters of design in the eyes of collectors – sets this slide projector apart from the rest. **£200-300**

SHOPPING GUIDE

Think of looking hip, think of shopping in London's Carnaby Street – the place to see and be seen in the 'Swinging Sixties'. Affordable boutique-style fashion took both male and female dressing to new heights. For the first time it was mass-market street-style in synthetic fabrics and non-exclusive couture creations which led the way. The fashion revolution centred on Carnaby Street from around 1964 helped, no doubt, by the fact that the Beatles and the Kinks openly shopped there. And of course it was the Kinks who sang about the 'Carnabetian Army' in their 1964 hit single 'Dedicated Follower of Fashion'. This guide by David Block showed the style-conscious where to buy. **£4**

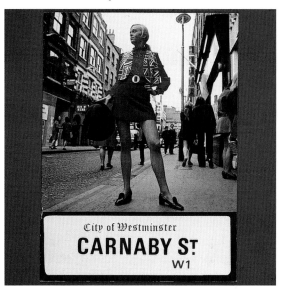

POLAROID 'SWINGER' CAMERA

If you owned a Polaroid 'Swinger' Land camera (1965), for taking instant black and white snaps, you were as swinging as the decade in which it was made! The adverts made a play for high-fashion girls sporting their new Land camera with the slogan, 'Meet the Swinger' underneath. Was it the girl or was it the camera; or was it both? Big sales, despite expensive film costs, suggested snap-happy youngsters fell for Polaroid-speak and American industrial designer, Henry Drefuss's (1904-72) young, contemporary styling. As with all cameras it's the condition that counts, check the case carefully for any splits in the plastic, chips or scratches. **£5-20**

PLASTIC ASHTRAY AND PENTRAY

This is style for the mass market. This plastic ashtray and pentray, designed to tackle old problems in a new way, was created by Austrian, Walter Zeischegg. He was a key lecturer at the Ulm Design College in West Germany (1955-68), who spent much of his time contemplating humble everyday objects, in particular thinking about how his designs would be used. As you can see practicality plays an important part here – the ashtray stacks and the pentray is large enough to neatly tidy away almost everything. Like the avant-garde Bauhaus school (1919-33), the lifespan of the Ulm College and its designs was relatively short hence the resurgence of interest in the group today. Both these pieces are clearly marked 'Helit-product' underneath with Zeischegg's name and a model number. **£70-90**

VALENTINE TYPEWRITER

You can hardly miss Italian designer Ettore Sottsass (b.1917) and British designer, Perry King's (b.1938) vibrant orange-red 'Valentine' typewriter for Olivetti (1969). The plan was that it would become the heart of every home (hence its name) no matter who bought it – young, old, rich or poor – and Sottsass's lavish launch ads showed precisely that. Dispensing with convention they styled a fun, fashionable Pop machine for a Pop age that was ideal anywhere 'except in an office, so as not to remind anyone of the monotonous working hours', according to Sottsass. The body was moulded out of bright ABS plastic, which was 'all in one with its handle [ingeniously attached at the back] and cover [which clipped to it]'. There was no sense of the Valentine being styled on the Japanese portables that were flooding the market at the time – this was radically different – 'An anti-machine machine', which went on to win a coveted Compasso d'Oro award for its design. Sottsass's romantic vision of a Valentine in every home was short-lived and after just eighteen months production stopped because it failed to find true mass-market appeal. As you can imagine those that were kept are popular collectables now. Check it carries Perry King's classic 'Valentine' graphics. **£100-200**

NIKON AND COLOUR SUPPLEMENTS

Just as home-style became more open-plan and relaxed so did photography. The mass of national newspaper colour supplements that sprang up in this decade (*The Sunday Times,* 1962, the *Sunday Telegraph,* 1964 and the *Observer,* 1965) waved 'goodbye' to the

formality of posed studio pictures, replacing them instead with a more relaxed and informal photographic style. Real life was the issue, as it happened, and fashion photographers like David Bailey (b. 1938) became renowned for their incisive portraits. The new breed chose Japanese tools, which helped to transform the camera market too. By 1962, Japan had replaced West Germany as the world's top producer of cameras. In war zones like Korea and Vietnam, where photojournalism conveyed the realities of conflict at the close of the decade, light automatic Japanese cameras won hands down. Advanced amateurs could only be inspired by the results of the Nikon F (introduced in 1959 but widely used in the sixties). Clever pricing meant they weren't beyond the keen photographer's reach. **£200+ (Nikon F) £5 (colour supplements)**

IT MAGAZINE

The controversial articles and graphic illustrations that appeared in the British magazine *International Times* (1966-71), which changed its name to *IT* after legal action from *The Times* newspaper, summed up the underground press of the sixties. They were strongly anti-establishment and championed peace, sexual liberation, subversive politics and legalized drugs. They were closely linked with psychedelia and the music world. For example *IT* was launched at a party at the Roundhouse, the venue where the band Pink Floyd (then dubbed *the* underground group) made its major debut. Issues carried adverts from Apple, the Beatles' company, and illustrations by Australian artist Martin Sharp who was behind some of the most famous album covers and posters of the sixties. Controversy eventually forced the magazine's closure – its limited run means that issues are now in demand, fuelled by recent museum interest. **£10-15**

OLYMPIC CIGARETTES

This was the decade when smoking was still viewed as film star cool! However, information was gradually trickling through about the harmful effects of tobacco on health, causing sales of filter-tipped brands like this to take off. Manufacturers like the British firm, W.A. & A.C Churchman (then part of the Imperial Tobacco Company, formed in 1901) made one of their lines stand out by linking it with sportsmen and the Olympics. Just the name on this packet, 'Olympic' (sold until 1967), conjures up a healthy, sporty image. Over 200 varieties existed, each with details of different sporting heroes printed on the back. This packet from 1961 focuses on Grand National winners.
£2-5

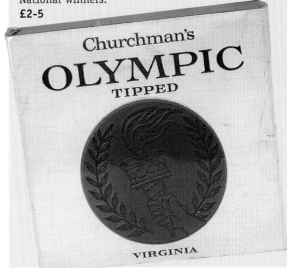

BOOMERANG DESK

The curvaceous outline of this 'Boomerang' desk showed how industrial fibreglass, traditionally used for prototypes, could be turned into both sculptural and functional furniture for the home. French sculptor, Maurice Calka was awarded the Grand Prix de Rome for this innovative piece of styling for French makers Leleu Deshay in 1969. Because they were only made in limited numbers few originals like this have survived, hence the price tag. **£10-14,000 (with an original chair the value can double)**

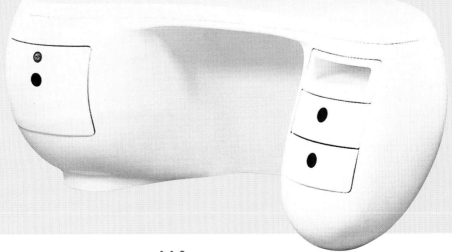

in the study

BOBY TROLLEY

The 'Boby' trolley by Italian designer, Joe Colombo (1930-71) showed how versatile shiny ABS plastic could be. From the man who brought us the all-in-one mini kitchen came this all-in-one home/office unit in 1970. It was tailor-made to slip neatly under any office desk with equally versatile storage compartments for pens, pencils, paper and files. If you needed more storage, simply increase its height by removing the pen tray and clipping another few sections on top. Colombo took his streamlined approach to household clutter one step further with his 'Livingcentre', shown after his premature death, at the 1972 exhibition of Italian Design in New York. To distinguish Colombo's design from others check for his moulded signature on the bottom shelf (the 'Boby' was first made by Kartell, with later, slightly cheaper editions being made by Bieffeplast).
£250-300

TOPO LAMP

Although the idea of a flexible hinged lamp was pioneered with the distinctive 'anglepoise' back in the thirties, four decades later it lacked that modern look. So Italian lighting manufacturer, Stilnova, called on compatriot Joe Colombo to style a simple-to-make contemporary lamp, for an upbeat home or office. In 1970 he came up with this, the 'Topo' lamp, with a skeleton arm (hollowed to hide the cable) supporting a pear-shaped shade. Not only could you adjust the height of the 'Topo', but Colombo also made it capable of revolving in a complete circle – thereby adding another dimension to its usefulness.
£250-350

POCKET CALCULATOR

Clive Sinclair (b.1940) was the British electronics genius behind the world's first pocket calculator: the Sinclair Executive (launched June 1972). Measuring just 5 x 2 x ⅓ inches and weighing a mere 2½ ounces, it was a cigarette-packet-sized revolution, freeing users from bulky, desk-bound versions that were mostly limited to mains power. 'See how easily it slips into a pocket,' read Sinclair's advertisements. 'The other pocket calculators,' it continued, 'fit neatly into your briefcase'. To us now, it seems very basic – with the only functions being addition, subtraction, multiplication and division – but to those who splashed out, spending £79.95 (+VAT) on one of these, it was a miniature electronics revolution in the palm of their hand. Sinclair's company, Sinclair Radionics (registered 1961), were proud that it used just 'four deaf aid batteries', which would last for 'several weeks' in normal use. In reality with it continually switched on, the red LED (light emitting diode) display used so much power that it only lasted for four to six hours. Another limitation was its nasty habit (if you forgot to turn it off) of heating up the batteries to the extent that they blew up! Needless to say these little difficulties were ironed out in successive models and overall it was a great achievement and a huge success, winning a Design Council Award and a place in the Museum of Modern Art, New York. Collectors admire the Executive for its sheer innovation. Importantly, this one still has its original wallet and instructions. **£100-150**

VERTEBRA CHAIR

Italian furniture giant Castelli's 'Vertebra' chair (from 1977) was clearly a major influence on home/office style. So much so, that even today it would be hard to find a desk chair that doesn't draw at least one or two ideas from Castelli's original. Appropriately titled, the 'Vertebra' was moulded to fit the shape of your spine. Designers Emilio Ambasz (b.1943) and Giancarlo Piretti (b.1940) were concerned with practical ergonomic solutions and their tilting adjustable chair was perfectly suited to most shapes. Importantly for Piretti, Director of Research and Design at Castelli, it was easy for his firm to mass-produce. As you can imagine originals like this are more sought-after than later issues and the only way of telling the two apart is obvious wear and tear! Just to confuse you, both will be marked 'Manufactured by Castelli'.
£300-500

OLIVETTI'S DIVISUMMA

You certainly knew you were in touch with modern technology when you felt the keypad of the Olivetti (founded 1911) 'Divisumma 18' calculator (1973). Alluringly tactile, its keys were sealed under a thin rubber skin that undulated like the craters on the moon (something widely seen thanks to Lunar Orbiter II's revolutionary photographs taken a few years earlier). Whether contemporary moon talk provided serious inspiration for Italian designer Mario Bellini (b.1935) remains unknown but he certainly took the humble desk calculator onto a new level, making it an attractive as well as functional piece of equipment. Condition is a factor here – the rubber skin and plastic body must be in good shape to attract a collector's eye – no cracking, chipping or fading. **£200**

BRAUN'S SLIDE PROJECTOR

German manufacturers Braun (founded 1921) brought us the first fully automatic, mass-produced slide projector back in the mid-fifties – a perfect fit for Kodak's new 35mm colour slide film. Two decades later in 1970 designer Robert Oberheim (b.1938) built on that success and followed Braun's classic styling with this D7 model – a unique design that combined a slide projector with a slide viewer. Clean lines, a quality German lens and an easy to use but rugged slide mechanism meant this was a product that was built to last. It's unusual to see an example like this still with its box and the original paper label, giving the model details underneath. **£100-150**

MINOLTA 110 ZOOM SLR

The Minolta 110 Zoom SLR was the first SLR (single lens reflex) camera for 110 film when it came out in 1976. Taking advantage of the popularity of cheap colour 110 cartridges, Minolta (founded 1928) promised to achieve a result that would rival conventional 35mm SLR cameras. The bonus here was that Minolta's version was half as heavy and, like 110 Instamatics, was extremely compact. Unfortunately, it wasn't cheap like its cousins and despite the flexibility of the fixed zoom lens over basic 110 models, the processed quality never really matched that of the larger format film. **£80**

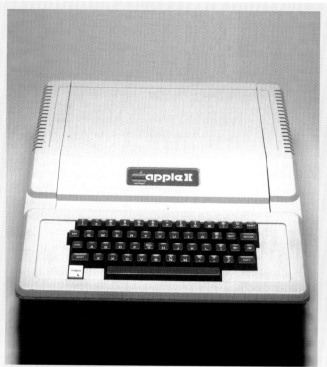

APPLE II

When the American Intel Corporation (founded 1968) launched the world's first microprocessor (the now legendary 4004) it ignited the personal computer revolution. It was almost unbelievable that a chip no larger than a thumbnail could be as powerful as the world's first electronic computer, ENIAC, built in 1946, which filled an entire room. There to take full advantage of the new microprocessor technology were two Americans, Steven Wozniak and Steven Jobs, and their Apple Computer company (founded 1976). This is their Apple II – the first personal computer to come in a plastic case with colour graphics (launched in 1977). It's remarkable to think that for the seriously expensive £1,000 price tag you could only type using capital letters – although the coloured screen was a bonus and it did come with built-in sound. Compared with today's technology though, the II was a fraction of the speed and positively basic – probably the reason why most were junked. Today they're like gold-dust and a computer collector's dream is a mint version with original software and manuals. **£200+**

'APTA SERIES' MINI-DESK

How useful to have a desk that folded up like a briefcase at the end of the day! That was exactly what modern design guru, Italian Giovanni ('Gio') Ponti (1891-1979) achieved with this 'Apta Series' mini-desk. Versatile, portable and ideal for not just one, but two, keen workers, you expected nothing less innovative from Ponti. After all, he was the architect and designer who styled Milan's Pirelli Tower (1956) and founded and edited the influential design magazine *Domus* (from 1928). This particular desk was never mass-produced making survivors relatively rare. **£4,000-5,000**

in the study

TELEPHONE CARDS

When British Telecom made life easier for all call-box users by introducing their very first telephone cards in 1981 they could not have anticipated that collectors would be so interested. In fact, credit-card-sized 'greenies' (the first issues) along with a host of colourful commemorative and advertising cards from telephone companies world-wide (including Mercury cards from 1988) have plenty of collector appeal long after they've been used. Only recently in a New Zealand auction, a trial phonecard changed hands amongst telegerists (telephone card collectors) for over £28,000. In Britain, interest took off when the first coloured BT issues began in 1986. It's a sort of modern-day alternative to stamp collecting and enthusiasts prize scarce issues, mistakes and mint condition examples. Knowing the lingo is a good starting point and learning about 'control numbers' is another. Pick up almost any used card designed to work with a phone's optical reading system and you'll spot a series of stamped numbers on the back – these will help you with dating. For instance, the first number, say 5, indicates the year – 1985 or 1995; the next two numbers, say 03, show the month – March, the letter in the middle is meaningless and the remaining five numbers are a guide to the quantity issued. If you're lucky you might be holding one of these BT London Challenge cards – one of the firm's early commercial issues briefly sold in 1987. **£550 (mint) £500 (used)**

SINCLAIR ZX80

Always keen to get there first, the enterprising Clive Sinclair (b.1940) started the eighties off with a bang when he launched the first truly affordable home computer – the ZX80 (in 1980). Aimed at beginners who wanted to take their first steps into the world of computing, the appealingly priced ZX80 (£99.95 ready assembled) seemed ideal. Sinclair Research designed a discrete user-friendly product that newcomers could use with their TV screen as the monitor. The electronics were housed in an instantly recognizable white plastic keyboard case that measured a mere 9 x 7 inches – far smaller than anything else on the market at the time. However the size itself proved a problem – the keys on the 'touch sensitive' membrane keypad were awkward to press. Also, when you did use the keyboard there was no response either in feel or sound to indicate that your selection had registered – no wonder it was called the 'dead flesh' keyboard by some users. Memory size was limited to a mere 1K – not enough to write a serious programme. So, realistically the only option was to upgrade with a top-heavy 16K RAM pack that plugged into the back. As one user recalls the classic 'ram pack wobble' was an annoying feature that meant you lost everything when the unbalanced peripheral decided to fall out. Compared to Sinclair's improved ZX81 (launched a year later), which sold on a mass-market sale, the ZX80 had far fewer followers. Many machines were simply thrown away in the course of an upgrade, so collectors class them as valuable gems today. It's difficult to find complete examples in good condition with the RAM pack and metallic paper printer. Watch out for the remains of chewing gum on the plug-in memory and the back of the white case – it was a popular way of avoiding the 'wobble'! **£100+**

Japanese photographic giant Konica (founded 1873) broke new ground this decade with their innovative A4 camera (1989). In the closing years of the seventies they'd already moved mountains in modern photography by launching the first auto-date imprinting system, followed by the world's first motorized auto-loading, auto-winding compact AE SLR camera. The eighties was a decade that pioneered compact technology and Konica's advances made the mighty A4 possible. At its launch, it was the smallest and lightest fully automatic auto-focus camera on the market. As a collectable it's earmarked for potential. Although die-hard camera fans are still wedded to earlier pieces, it won't be long before the value of this little clicker starts to climb. **£15-25**

SINCLAIR 'SPECTRUM'

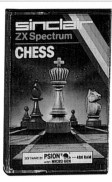

Hot on the heels of Sinclair Research's ZX81 computer was the firm's 'Spectrum' model with a new type of rubber membrane keyboard, colour graphics and basic sound thanks to its integral piezo buzzer. The Spectrum first appeared in April 1982 priced at £125, as the next stage in Sinclair's personal computer system. Although it became a best-seller in the home computer market, it tended to be sidelined as a games machine rather than a serious computing tool, consequently Sinclair lost out to rival Acorn as the BBC Microcomputer for schools. Spectrum models in good condition like this, complete with the Microdrive accessory, are becoming hard to find. The most sought-after are the first run of machines (issue 1) with the distinctive light grey rubber key mat. **£250**

ATARI 800 KL MACHINE

Thanks to an explosion of interest in computer games in the eighties there was a surge in demand for cheap home computers like this Atari 800 KL machine – an updated version of the firm's (est. 1972) first foray into the personal computer market in the late seventies. Good graphics and sound meant it was ideal for home versions of arcade favourites like the highly addictive 'Pong' (a simple but ingenious screen-based bat and ball contest), which were sold in plug-in cartridge form. Although the Atari 800 was intended as a programmable computer for serious work, like Sinclair's Spectrum it was mainly used for gaming. Today an ever-growing number of computer collectors are searching for pristine versions of both machine and games. The latter were remarkably expensive in their day, the simpler ones retailing at an average of £20 each in 1983. **£10-15**

PHONEBOOK ANSWERING MACHINE

The phonebook answering machine blended advanced eighties electronics with slick YUPPIE styling by building on the phenomenally successful Filofax formula. American designer, Lisa Krohn (b. 1963) came up with the concept in 1986 whilst still a student. With the help of established designer, Tucker Viemeister (b. 1948 – famous for those wacky Joe Boxer watches), Krohn turned what could have been a complex machine into an easy-to-use home/office help. By simply flipping the 'pages' you switched from one group of functions to another. Although it was never commercially produced, design collectors are still interested in award-winning prototypes like this. One reason for this is that the phonebook answering machine was way ahead of its time. The designers hoped that it would be able to use voice recognition technology, so it could print out a transcript of the caller's message. Sadly we're still awaiting the technology necessary to make this a reality! **£500+**

MICKEY MOUSE TELEPHONE

This colourful Mickey Mouse telephone made by British electronics giant Plessey first appeared as part of Post Office Telecommunications' new line of rental telephones. A year later it appeared as part of their Special Range of telephones that you could buy rather than rent, when British Telecom was formalised in the early eighties. After years of rigid restrictions and limitations on design and colour, it was quite clear that the high-flying eighties had arrived with a flurry. 'This loveable cartoon character can bring an extra smile to your telephone calls,' said the BT advertisements. However, with a £120 price tag plus line rental, it's unlikely that those who enjoyed the 'talk with Mickey' experience had much to laugh about! **£40-60**

CORDLESS SWATCH TELEPHONE

It oozes nineties style, is provocatively sexy and has select market appeal – all hallmarks that go to make this cordless Swatch (est. 1978) telephone a collectors' gem. When it first appeared in our stores in 1997 this bit of equipment simply stood out because it broke with tradition. There's a trio of groovy opaque colours for the plastic handsets, which are conveniently interchangeable. Then there's the telephone's style – a sensual handset that's so comfortably curved you don't want to put it down and a base that holds it upright and ready for use. But it doesn't stop here, strip away the exterior and inside there's modern digital technology from German firm Siemens (est. 1847). As a collectable the Swatch telephone is destined to succeed because it mirrors the era in terms of design, materials (moulded plastic) and technology. It also helps that it's a fairly pricey product sold in a competitive market, meaning that only the bold are likely to own one. Swatch isn't keen to see the telephone's retail price discounted (after all it would cheapen what they've created) and there are less expensive and less glamorous alternatives out there. So the Swatch telephone is going to be a select market seller that's worth keeping – in its box of course! Look out for the first releases, without the Alpha text around the numbered buttons. **£109.99**

CANON IXUS POCKET CAMERA

It's hard to believe that a quality camera with the equivalent of a 35-70mm zoom lens can shrink to the size of a cigarette packet and fit in the top pocket of your shirt. But the Ixus – Canon's tiny pocket camera (launched 1996), does exactly that. The rugged stainless steel body conceals a maze of minute circuitry for the very latest processing technology – APS (the Advanced Photo System). 'There's a more detailed information exchange between camera and film,' say those clever designers at Canon, which translates to mean finer quality printing from a compact camera. Therefore, it's no surprise that the Ixus has already been selected for exhibition in London's Design Museum. A flash of nineties innovation worth holding onto. **£180**

in the study

'DAUPHINE' CALCULATOR

As personal organizers and PCs take over our lives, the days of adding up with a humble calculator seem numbered. But the 'Dauphine' is far from a dying breed. It's a classy calculating machine from Italian design giant, Alessi, (from 1997) under the umbrella of great styling from Sowden Design. The combination of good looks and functionality means this adds up well for the future. **£44**

'HOMER' HOME/OFFICE STORAGE UNIT

Designed to be a 'home' for whoever uses it, the aptly named 'Homer' is a personal home/office storage unit that's infinitely mobile. Slick styling from a happening British design team (PearsonLloyd, est. 1997) plus versatility and contemporary colours make the Homer a bright solution for today's workers. Knoll International (whose fifties and sixties pieces are already serious collectors' treasures) launched Homer in 1997. Like a chameleon, it adapts to suit its surroundings: in the study it's a discreet storage-cum-work unit with a fully rotational, height adjustable top – a sort of briefcase on wheels, colour coded, lockable and personalized with a slot for your business card. When you're in, simply wheel it over and it tucks under Knoll's PL1 desk furniture. When you're out, remove it, park it and leave the area free for something else. **£452+**

APPLE IMAC

Another revolutionary idea from Apple – the firm that ignited the personal computer revolution in the seventies. The iMac is a modern machine designed for global communication in the 21st century. It's speedy with integrated Internet access; it's ultra stylish with a smooth, all-in-one design and most noticeably it's striking with a bright coloured plastic case – no wonder the iMac (launched 1998) has become the most popular computer in America. Against the mass of dull grey and brown conventional PCs, it's been held up as a great design achievement on countless occasions. However, the launch of five new colours in January 1999 means the original bondi-blue iMac like this, is the one to keep. It may not be as fast as its newcomer cousins, but it is the first in the iMac line. The fruity colours (Strawberry, Lime, Blueberry, Tangerine and Grape) are intended to replace the bondi-blue version, so the lifespan of this version is sure to be short. If you own one, hang on to it – if you don't, invest in one for the future, complete with manuals and accessories of course! **£679**

PSION SERIES 5 HANDHELD COMPUTER

The British firm Psion (founded 1980) launched the world's first handheld computer in 1984. This Series 5 marks a new step in computer design – a high-powered processor is wrapped up in a tiny body that weighs little more than 360g (13 ounces) in total. In spite of its size, clever design makes it easy to use with a slide out keyboard that's the best in its category. Its ergonomic design has won the Series 5 countless awards and contributed to its selection by the Design Council as one of the forward-thinking Millennium Products. The model to keep is this special edition pearlescent series 5 in aqua green – a luxury version complete with a matching mulberry case. A sure bet if ever I saw one! **£449.95**

RECYCLED PENCILS

In an age where environmental concerns have highlighted limited resources, it's recycled products that are leading the way into the future. Don't let your eyes deceive you – these recycled pencils are made from just some of the four billion polystyrene cups that are thrown away annually. 'Thousands of acres of forest are clear-felled every year to make pencils. That doesn't have to happen,' says the brain behind these potential collectables, Edward Douglas-Miller of Remarkable Pencils. Using his chemistry background he's worked out a way to create a plastic-based pencil shell that behaves like wood and can even be sharpened. It's interesting to think that you're writing with something that you once used to drink from – but how many of us will be astute enough to resist using these for scribbling? Like the Psion, the Design Council has already plucked these as well-designed gems for the Millennium. So prepare for these pencils to write a new chapter in collecting! **30p each**

BAYGEN FREEPLAY SELF-POWERED TORCH

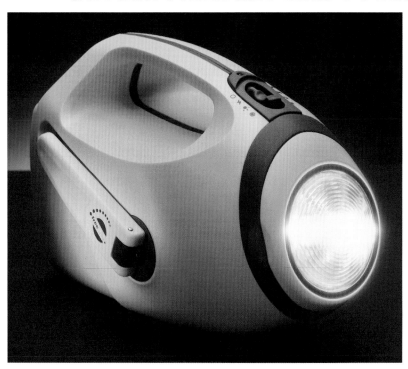

Super smooth design, great colour and novel technology from the firm that brought us the world's first wind-up radio (the BayGen Power Group, est. 1994), are evident in the BayGen Freeplay Self-Powered Torch. It's a handy collectable that you won't want to put down. Twenty seconds of winding gives you four minutes of light and when that runs out you simply wind it up again. Plucked out in one recent exhibition as a 'Design Icon of the 20th Century' – this torch's potential shines bright. However, rumour has it that a 'new improved' version is set to strike, which may be good for the stranded motorist but won't be so great as a collectable. As far as collectability goes, it's the first of a run like this that counts! **£49.99**

in the living room

IN THE

Living Room

After the separations of wartime, peacetime reunited Britain's families who started afresh in the 'new Elizabethan age' with modern-style living. Bomb-damaged terraces were exchanged for post-war New Towns and modern housing leapt ahead with alternative room layouts. Gone was the idea of separate sitting and eating spaces, instead fifties housing unveiled the 'all-purpose living-room' for coffee mornings, TV dinners and showing off to guests.

A fashionable 'living room' came with composition flooring (cork tiles or shiny linoleum), softened by a rug, pale-papered walls, oodles of ornaments and flexible space-saving furniture to add elements of contemporary style. However, the ultimate accessory, if you could afford it, was a 'television receiver', which, according to the manufacturers, when positioned 'one side or other of the fireplace' integrated beautifully as an item of furniture in its own right.

So the focus of the living room shifted from roaring fire to flickering screen, giving the wireless a back seat in the process. Seating was arranged in an 'L' or 'U' shape to accommodate the whole family who gathered round to watch programmes, and from 1955 – when independent television hit the screen – advertisements. Manufacturers took advantage of the surge in demand for sets and fifties living rooms became home to aptly branded TV lamps ('for easy viewing in subdued lighting'), TV chairs and even tasty TV-time biscuits.

The organic asymmetry that had shaped fifties home-style gave way to a fascination for geometry in the sixties. Televisions and radios reflected the passion for spheres, which after 1969 became linked with the Space-helmet look. Futuristic action/adventure series like *The Prisoner* brought state of the art furniture like Eero Aarnio's classic 'Globe' chair into the home. To make certain that you knew what to buy a new breed of lifestyle magazines and newspaper colour supplements reinforced the contemporary look.

The harnessing of plastics that had played such a role in furniture design in the sixties was taken a stage further in the early seventies by Italian designers who led the way in interior style. Although much of what they unveiled at the influential 'New Domestic Landscape' exhibition in 1972 was highly conceptual, some elements did filter through on to high-street furnishings. Many of their ideas, especially in the field of moulded plastic, were curtailed by the Oil Crisis, which caused the price of a raw material that had been affordable to spiral out of control.

This meant a return to nature in the seventies living room, a mix and match look with natural woods, leathers and a sprinkling of antique pieces. Singer, Petula Clark paraded the latest living room style in her advertisements for interiors firm, Sandersons.

By the eighties patterns had disappeared in favour of bright, clinically white living space as a showcase for the vivid furniture inside. Traditional styles were re-worked in a modern way and in 1988 *Design Magazine* talked of 'cool, simple and adaptable' living room furniture. Chairs, sofas and coffee tables were again made from solid industrial materials, this time sheet glass and forged steel. The less-cluttered look was 'in' and made a perfect backdrop for the crystal clear stackable hi-fi systems that became a major leisure preoccupation of the eighties.

In the nineties colour is everywhere, whether it is soft and subtle for a 'cool, contemporary feel' or 'rich, vivid and dramatic' for a retro-inspired look. Against this revival in vibrancy is an array of furniture as multi-purpose as the living space it graces. Much of the inspired design is by a group of key 'Cool Britannia' names whose work has taken the world by storm. In 1998 their talent was highlighted at the ground-breaking Powerhouse: UK show and elements of that styling have filtered down to the high street. Nothing is quite what it seems in the nineties living room; chairs can be tables, lights can be stools and there's no such thing as a plain old sofa. The textural look is back with hand-woven carpets and a revival in patterned wallpapers. Yet, for a decade steeped in the past, modern furnishing style cuts into the future using fresh new materials.

Spindly-legged plant pot stands like this were a stylish way of bringing nature into the home. With a careful bit of positioning, the green leaves of a rubber plant and its conical stand could break up those monotonous lines of solid inter-war furniture. As decorating with indoor plants grew in popularity (hand-in-hand with flower arranging), a host of textiles and ceramics turned fashionable by incorporating plant stand motifs. Terence Conran (b. 1931) styled his own version and used it in his 'Plant Life' pattern for Midwinter in 1956. Enid Seeney also used plant stand motifs in her 'Homemaker' ceramics series for Ridgway in 1957.

£350 (Conran basketweave stand)

All-enveloping comfort and flowing organic style were behind Arne Jacobsen's (1902-71) 'Egg Chair'. It was fiercely modern, not only in its look but also in its materials (a moulded plastic shell, latex foam upholstery glued in place and a cover that fitted like a glove in leather, fabric or, in this case, vinyl). It was originally intended for hotel use (in Stockholm's Royal SAS Hotel), but sheer comfort and futuristic style made these pieces perfect for an up-to-date domestic setting.

£750 (egg chair)

These vibrant Venini vases from Italy were shockingly different. Fulvio Bianconi (1915-96), the talented illustrator and caricaturist known for his much copied 'handkerchief' or 'fazzoletto' vases, which are still made today, designed them. Here, complex glassmaking methods create a fresh new look. On the left, his 'Pezzato' (patchwork) vase is made from fused rectangular panels of coloured glass (1951). His 'Scozzese' (Scottish) vase, on the right, has a latticework of encased coloured threads to simulate tartan fabric. Period originals have soared in value recently – acid etched signatures are typical of these rather than the engraved and dated signatures found on today's reproductions.

£2,500 ('Pezzato') £6,500 ('Scozzese')

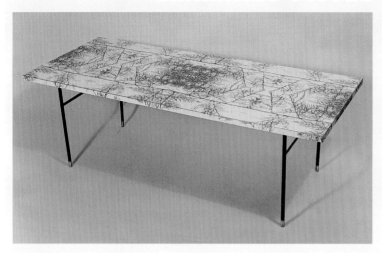

Easy-clean laminate-topped tables were fitting for a decade that valued the simulated plastic look more than the real thing! But if you yearned for a synthetic that was truly stylish British designer Terence Conran captured the outline of real leaves and ferns on the laminate surface (in the case of Wareite). Infinitely mobile, tables such as these were ideally suited to those who had changed the focal point of their living room from the fireplace to the television. Drawn up to within arm's reach of the set, they made family TV dinners far more manageable. **£75**

Lucienne Day (b. 1917) has to be Britain's foremost post-war textile designer. Scooped up and commissioned by Heals (founded 1810) she first achieved notoriety in 1951 at the Festival of Britain with her celebrated 'Calyx' design. It was the perfect complement to husband Robin's forward-looking furniture and was full of movement and vitality – a marked contrast to the staid colours and designs promoted by the wartime Utility Scheme. Needless to say 'Calyx' went on to win a host of international design awards. Original 'Calyx' linen fabric is scarce because it was never sold on a mass-market scale. **£1,500**

Robin Day's (b.1915) light-framed but supportive lounger armchair (1952) became an icon of modern home-style. It was one of the early pieces to come out of his successful partnership with the English furniture firm S. Hille & Co. Day's recliner was seen as aspirational by many, (hence it's rarity value today). This piece achieved mass recognition when Enid Seeney incorporated a stylised version of it in her 'Homemaker' pattern. **£1,500**

Babycham, 'the genuine champagne perry' had a real aura of feminine sophistication about it when it appeared in 1953. Showerings Ltd (est. 1932), the British drinks manufacturer, took a traditional pear cider and transformed it into the first fashionable young girls' party drink. Beauty contests at Britain's booming holiday camps promoted an inspirational image of Miss Babycham – the girl you could be like, providing you chose the right beverage. The frolicking baby deer confirmed it all – a character that came to life like the drink itself with Babycham's animated television advertisements. The recent re-launch of Babycham by Matthew Clark Brands Ltd has revived interest. Watch out for fake Carlton Ware Babycham figures (without the original plinths), carrying false marks. **£4 (babycham figure) £5 (glass)**

The biggest public event of the decade was undoubtedly the Queen's Coronation on 2 June 1953. Post-war Britain sunk its heart and soul into street celebrations and commemoratives. For the first time the BBC's television coverage was broadcast all day long (without the usual breaks). As you can imagine, thousands of mugs, cups, saucers and plates were hurried into production to meet demand – and most of them are still cherished nearly fifty years on! However, it's the less common commemoratives that have more than a token value today. This Wedgwood Coronation tankard is one that stands out. It uses a modern design that wartime artist Eric Ravilious (1903-42) originally created for the proposed Coronation of Edward VIII. The fact that it was priced beyond the average pocket limited sales and added to its rarity. **£200**

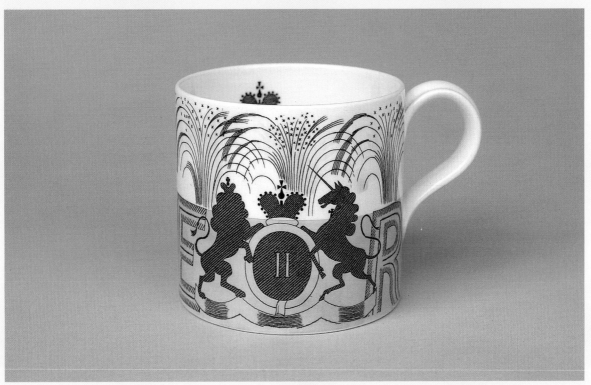

The curvaceous 'Cloud' table by Scottish designer Neil Morris (b.1918) was another way of bringing natural, organic shapes into the home whilst saving precious raw materials at the same time. Not only was its undulating outline ideal for snuggling up to an armchair, there was a valuable saving to be made on the quantity of laminated plywood needed (a material traditionally used for aeroplane prototypes). Although Morris's table appeared in the late forties, the 'Cloud' design lasted well into the fifties with the help of rival versions. Stores like Heals advertised something similar at this time, with a nest of four boomerang tables tucked underneath. If you want Morris's original, look out for H. Morris & Co. Ltd printed marks under the tabletop. **£400**

Fifties home entertainment saw the radio take a back seat in favour of television. Furniture in the living room was re-orientated so that the focal point for the family was their black and white screen. Advertisers and product manufacturers quickly realized its influence and a line of TV-related products were hurried into production. Alongside TV lamps and chairs were delicious TV biscuits like these made by Crawfords. No TV dinner was complete without them. **£33**

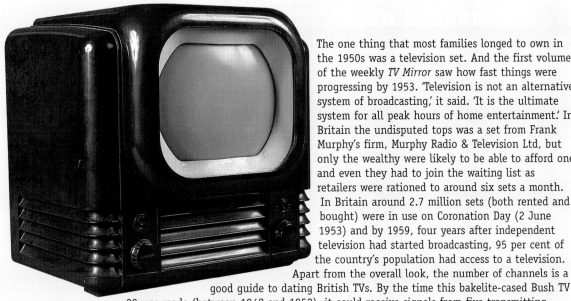

The one thing that most families longed to own in the 1950s was a television set. And the first volume of the weekly *TV Mirror* saw how fast things were progressing by 1953. 'Television is not an alternative system of broadcasting,' it said. 'It is the ultimate system for all peak hours of home entertainment.' In Britain the undisputed tops was a set from Frank Murphy's firm, Murphy Radio & Television Ltd, but only the wealthy were likely to be able to afford one and even they had to join the waiting list as retailers were rationed to around six sets a month. In Britain around 2.7 million sets (both rented and bought) were in use on Coronation Day (2 June 1953) and by 1959, four years after independent television had started broadcasting, 95 per cent of the country's population had access to a television. Apart from the overall look, the number of channels is a good guide to dating British TVs. By the time this bakelite-cased Bush TV 22 was made (between 1948 and 1952), it could receive signals from five transmitting stations plus repeaters, which rapidly expanded to thirteen by 1954-5 and then seventeen and twenty-one as the countrywide network improved. **£150-200**

The fifties was a decade of revolution for radio. Despite its overall poor quality, crowds flocked to buy the cream-painted FB10 – the aptly named 'Toaster' – from Kent-based, Kolster Brandes Ltd. This Bakelite version that was anything but dull was priced at a fraction of Murphy's wooden equivalents. No wonder it was the first popular British radio to reach a million sales. Those who fancied the American look could opt for blue or red cases (now precious because few listeners were prepared to pay the extra £1). A real boost for radio came from the tiny electronic components that replaced vacuum tubes – transistors. Because they were minute themselves and relied on far smaller batteries, workings and cases could be shrunk. The world's first transistor radio, the American TR-1 (1954) was living proof, measuring a mere 5 x 3 inches. **£50-60 (ivory) £150+ (blue or red)**

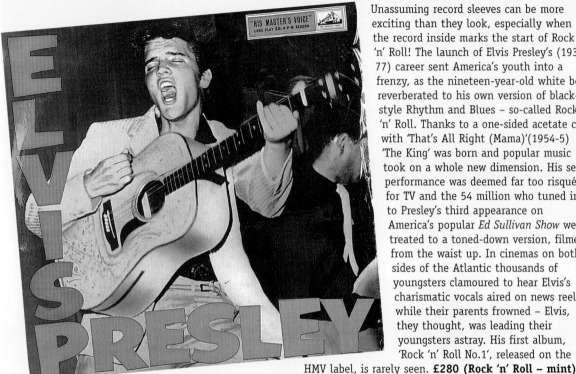

Unassuming record sleeves can be more exciting than they look, especially when the record inside marks the start of Rock 'n' Roll! The launch of Elvis Presley's (1935-77) career sent America's youth into a frenzy, as the nineteen-year-old white boy reverberated to his own version of black-style Rhythm and Blues – so-called Rock 'n' Roll. Thanks to a one-sided acetate cut with 'That's All Right (Mama)'(1954-5) 'The King' was born and popular music took on a whole new dimension. His sexy performance was deemed far too risqué for TV and the 54 million who tuned in to Presley's third appearance on America's popular *Ed Sullivan Show* were treated to a toned-down version, filmed from the waist up. In cinemas on both sides of the Atlantic thousands of youngsters clamoured to hear Elvis's charismatic vocals aired on news reels while their parents frowned – Elvis, they thought, was leading their youngsters astray. His first album, 'Rock 'n' Roll No.1', released on the HMV label, is rarely seen. **£280 (Rock 'n' Roll – mint)**

Hip fifties teenagers keen to break away from their parents' tastes found solace in popular music. Listening and dancing to it was their way of expressing their individualism and rebellious defiance. So thousands tuned into the weekly Top Twenty run down on pirate radio station Luxembourg's 'Pop Wavelength' – 208. Milk and coffee bars were the places to be seen and to catch up on the latest jukebox plays. Thanks to record players like this 'Deccalian' (which were more likely to belong to parents rather than their children) those hot new releases could be played back at home. It was designed by Harvey Schwarz for Decca Records Co. Ltd. and was one of the first British players to cater for the 7-inch 45 rpm (singles), the new 12-inch, 33 rpm – long plays (LPs) and extended plays (EPs) as well as the old 78s. Schwarz presented the innovative three-speed technology in a familiar way, basing his styling on a portable wind-up gramophone with an integral speaker. When it was aired at the Festival of Britain in 1951 it was clearly something very different that became a blueprint for player design that decade **£450+**

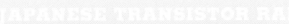

JAPANESE TRANSISTOR RADIO

This was the decade that saw radio take a back seat for the first time in 40 years. Although the wireless was still essential for most homes, listening habits had changed. Instead of gathering around it to hear the latest shows, radio played out a very different role now; as background entertainment in the living room, the garden, the kitchen or, for the youngsters, on the beach. Cheap mass-produced transistor sets were great pieces of party kit and the youth market snapped them up. This Japanese Ajax 'Serenade' (one of the growing number of foreign imports) was just the thing for the back of a Lambretta scooter, as its colourful box shows. **£20**

KNOLL ASSOCIATES TABLE

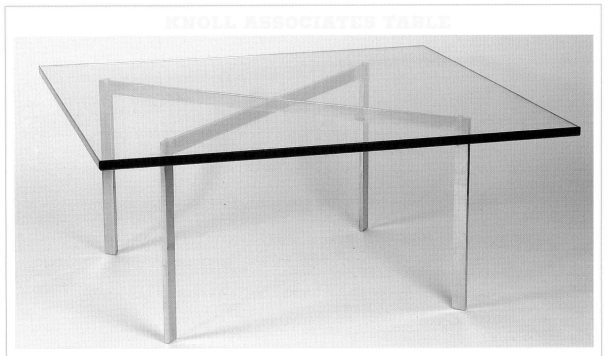

The clean lines of modern sixties architecture crept into homes with tables like this. Think of any architect-designed house of the decade and this table seems to echo its style. That's because the American firm who made it, Knoll Associates (est. 1933), worked with key figures from the world of architecture and design to create original modern furniture that directly reflected those new modern interiors. Occasional tables like this were seen in the Knoll showrooms as well as the pages of the contemporary design bible, *Studio International,* who confirmed Knoll's view that 'furniture must be related to the place it is to occupy'. If you weren't lucky enough to know a designer or his wealthy friends who would have owned something like this, you'd have brushed past similar tables in airport lounges or office foyers. Today collectors value them for their style. **£350**

WHITEFRIARS' BARK VASES

Whitefriars' (est. 1834) range of cylindrical bark vases and glasses (from 1967) not only looked good but felt good too. They captured the mood for textural decoration by blowing the glass into metal moulds made from real bark. This spark of innovation came to designer Geoffrey Baxter after wandering through the woods of North London. At first the colour options were limited to reddish brown (branded 'cinnamon'), greyish green ('willow') and inky blue ('indigo'). But other bright colours like 'kingfisher blue' and 'tangerine' appeared in 1969. The textural theme was widely copied by other firms, so spotting Whitefriar's can be difficult because there are no maker's marks to go by. As a guideline, look out for rich colouring and weighty pieces – it was always a quality hand-crafted production. **£68**

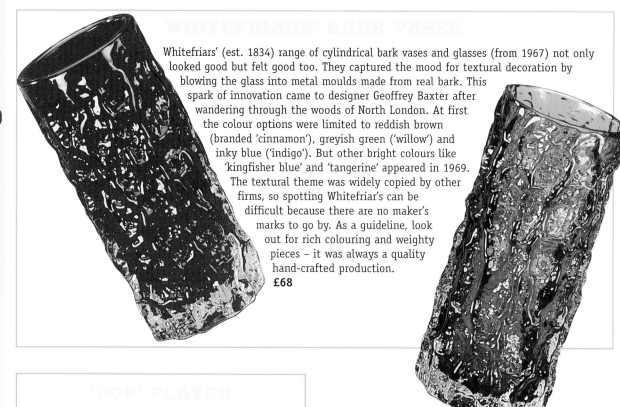

'POP' PLAYER

Modern sixties bedsits were incomplete without a record player. And few designs captured the swinging sixties more than Italian Mario Bellini's 'Pop' player for Grundig (1968). Light, easy to use (simply slip in a single and pop down the handle) and most importantly, portable, this was a teen dream. The brightly coloured plastic case (sold in a range of hues) was sculpted to look more like a must-have fashion accessory than a conventional record player. So it's no wonder that countless Beatles singles were heard (albeit muffled) blaring out of this little gem. **£200**

HANS COPER

While mass-produced ceramics of the decade followed a new cylindrical line, studio potters experimented with waisted shapes and tough glazes. Hans Coper (1920-81) was at the forefront of the resulting look which, as you can see from these two vases, was extremely sculptural and could be nothing other than handcrafted. Just a glance and it's easy to understand why they're commonly called 'dog-bone' or 'hourglass' vases. Because Coper was a perfectionist who destroyed anything that he felt wasn't 'up to scratch', his work is rare and sells for a premium today – look for his prized 'HC' seal on the base. **£6,300 (each)**

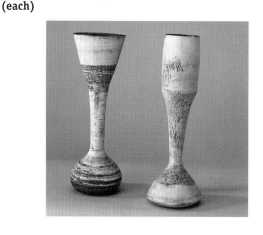

CHURCHILL COMMEMORATIVE

The death of Sir Winston Churchill (1874-1965), Britain's great wartime leader and former Prime Minister, on 24 January 1965 prompted a massive show of public grief. An estimated 300,000 people filed past his coffin as it lay in state in Westminster Hall and more than 350 million people in Europe watched the funeral service, on 30 January, on television. Apart from hundreds of newspaper and magazine souvenir editions (the majority worth under £5), commemoratives included this 'Churchill Plate' by Spode. Churchilliana (the name given to all memorabilia associated with Churchill) is avidly collected by those fascinated with his life story and political achievements. So a limited edition plate like this (one of only 5,000 made), still in its original gilt printed box would find plenty of keen buyers now. **£140**

'GLOBE/BALL' CHAIR

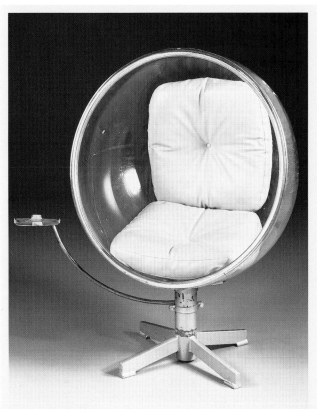

This moulded spherical lounger, the 'Globe' or 'Ball' chair – designed by Finn Eero Aarnio (b. 1932) and made by Asko in 1965 – played out its role in the futuristic action/adventure series *The Prisoner* (first aired on British TV in 1967). Perhaps it was the mysterious way that it rose from an underground chamber to reveal No.2, 'The Village's' administrator, which made it a key piece for forward-looking sixties homes and offices. A variety of options was available; from plastic shells in violent primaries to this clear model, complete with telephone platter – a special order from the BASF headquarters in Holland. Some of these cocooned micro-environments – perfect for a real couch potato – even came with integral speakers. **£1,500-2,000**

PLEASE PLEASE ME ★ THE BEATLES

PARLOPHONE

THE BEATLES

PLEASE PLEASE ME

with Love Me Do
and 12 other songs

THE BEATLES' 'PLEASE, PLEASE ME'

They may have started life as just another of Liverpool's 'beat' groups, but by 1962 The Beatles were Britain's hottest pop sensation. At the end of the recording session for their second single ('Please, Please Me') George Martin, Parlophone's (part of EMI) producer, knew he'd struck gold. Pressing the intercom button he announced perceptively, 'Gentleman, you have just made your first number one.' This mono recording of their first album, 'Please, Please Me' (1963) is prized because it's one of the few issued on Parlophone's gold and black label – a hang-over from the fifties. It was replaced weeks later by the more familiar yellow and black label. For record aficionados these are all classic vinyls made at a time when quality recording, then in its infancy thanks to stereo, was really taking off. In the early sixties stereo records and players started life as expensive luxuries so, compared with mono, far fewer sold. However, by the end of the decade and well into the next, stereo recordings were more commonplace and mono became a rarity. A serious bonus for all vinyl collectors are autographs – having the bands' signatures plastered somewhere either on the sleeve or label can turn a £5 record into a £500-plus gem.
£120-150 (mono album) £2,000 (mint condition stereo)

It may look like a mint imperial sweet but the Gardenegg chair was a slick piece of modern design – ideal for seventies entertaining, indoor or out. Light, portable and multifunctional, the plastic lid flipped open to make a cushioned seat, which was removable, for washing. Peter Ghyczy designed the Gardenegg in 1968 for Reuter, but the design lasted well into the seventies – this one is actually stamped underneath with the date, '23 April 1971'. Because many found their way onto the patio, do check their condition, weathering and neglect has meant re-painting, which reduces their value. **£400-600**

Hi-fi (high fidelity) equipment was gradually finding a place in a growing number of households keen to listen to quality, naturalistic audio. Thanks to transistor amplifiers those cabinet-sized radiograms of the fifties and sixties were shrunk into more compact systems. Improved stereo quality plus the wider availability of stereo records also made modern systems more appealing. Top-of-the-range manufacturers used innovative designer styling to set their luxury equipment apart from the rest. For example, Brionvega brought in Italian Mario Bellini to style their 'Totem' Hi-fi (1971). The speakers could either be swung out or detached and distanced for a better stereo effect. When the 'Totem' wasn't in use you could simply swing the speakers back to end up with a discreet white cube. **£1,500**

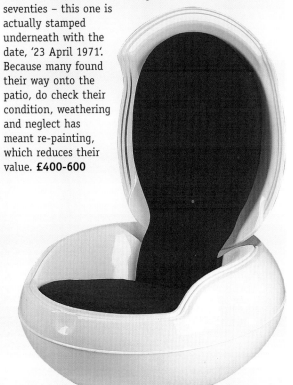

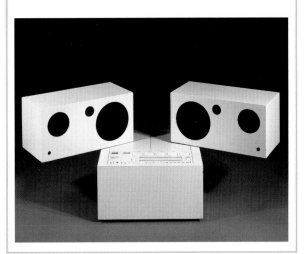

Fashionable and functional, the Japanese Panapet 70 radio from National Panasonic (one of the giant Matsushita Electric Company's brands formed in 1918) came in five 'crazy colours'. Shrinking transistor technology meant that products down-sized so much that in the case of this Panapet (sold 1972-4) you could hang it from your waist. **£25**

Italian designers set the pace for much of seventies homestyle. Thanks to international shows like 'Italy: The New Domestic Landscape; Achievements and Problems of Italian Design', a major contemporary and retrospective exhibition staged in New York (1972), the new-wave Italian look came under the spotlight. But two diverse design camps existed – the Modernists who put function and rationalism first and the radical Anti-Modernists (bonded by the 'Studio Alchimia' and later the 'Memphis' group) who were more conceptual and alternative, mocking the elitism of design. Clever mocking of the modernists in their own work was their way of popularizing design. This 'Sinvola da tavolo' lamp (1979) is by Michele de Lucci (b.1951) whose hat pins (rather alternative design materials) play games with conventional notions. Museums have been snapping up key seventies pieces like this for a while. If you can live with them the time is right for you to do the same. **£1,600**

You can see by the shape of the JVC videosphere TV (1970) that it was clearly influenced by the success of the Apollo mission to the moon the previous year. **£250**

Commemoratives made for the Queen's Silver Jubilee in 1977 easily outnumber anything made for Princess Anne's marriage in 1973. Street parties fuelled royal fever and everyone had to have something as a reminder – whether it was a pencil costing seven pence or an elegant bowl priced close to £5,000. Mugs carrying any one of the six officially licensed transfers and a host of unofficial images of the Queen are probably the most common item you'll see today. But don't expect these to be worth much more than £3 as we've all got one tucked away at the back of our cupboard. It's high-quality transfer printed tankards like this one made by Spode that are worth keeping. Originally it was sold in a red box, priced at £14.80. Don't worry if the box has disappeared, as collectors will still prize it. **£50**

This boxing glove chair seems to be Swiss design company, DeSede's, response to the idea of a modern-day chaise longue. It was a spirited seventies way of using the leather for which DeSede were famous. Those who lounged on the boxing glove could happily coo because they had something in common with Rolls-Royce and Bentley owners – DeSede provided sumptuous leather for their car interiors. The fact that you probably had to own a luxury limousine to be able to afford a cutting-edge design like this didn't seem to hamper sales. However, surprisingly few of these chairs are around today, making those that have survived seriously prized. **£5,000-6,000**

THE EAGLES

Along with Fleetwood Mac, The Eagles were among the most influential bands of the seventies. 'Hotel California' (1976) was the album that struck a chord with cool car cruisers all over the world. After a spell as Linda Ronstadt's backing group, the American band decided to go it alone and released their first album, 'The Eagles' in 1972. But it's the mixture of Don Henley's vocals with Joe Walsh's rhythmic guitar on 'Hotel California's' opening track (of the same name) that brought rock, folk and country fans together. Even in mint condition you wouldn't expect to pay more than £5 for this stereo album, but this one is a little different. All the band members (Don Felder, Glenn Frey, Don Henley, Randy Meisner and Joe Walsh) have signed the cover, which not surprisingly pushes the value up. **£250-300**

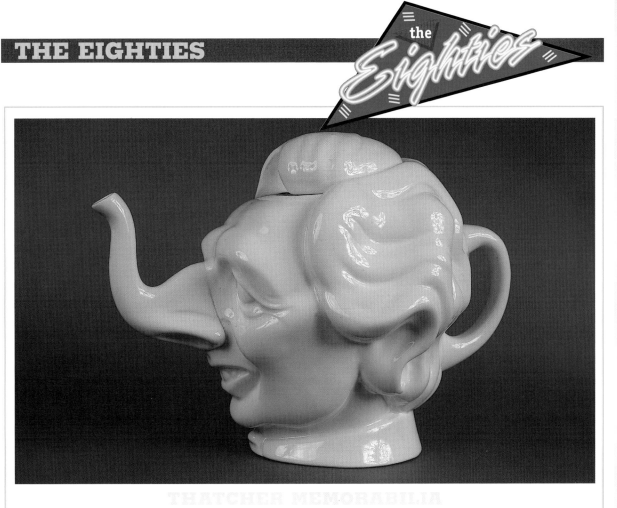

THATCHER MEMORABILIA

Margaret Thatcher, Britain's first woman Prime Minister (after the Conservative victory in 1979), was one of the most influential figures of the eighties. In line with the controversy that dogged her government, most memorabilia was based on caricature images, which far outsold any more reverent commemorative pieces. Fluck and Law – the men behind the hit satirical TV comedy show *Spitting Image* – designed a series of caricature Thatcher egg cups, mugs and tea pots for Carlton Ware. Then they were simply comical anti-establishment pieces, now they're sought after collectables. **£175**

'HOW HIGH THE MOON' CHAIR

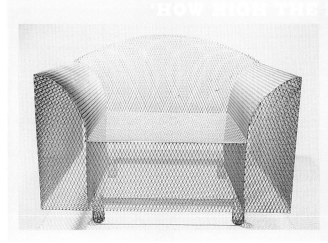

Japanese designer Shiro Kuramata also used an everyday industrial material, steel, for his mesh-like 'How High The Moon' chair (1986). Converted warehouse apartments – such a feature of eighties high-tech living – were the perfect fit for his designs, which were also seen in fashion designer Issey Miyake's shops. Like their surroundings, Kuramata's 'How High The Moon' chairs are curiously open, light and almost seemed to float ethereally upwards, thanks to his use of expanded steel. But measuring almost a metre square, these chairs demanded serious space, so they were never mass market living-room sellers. **£3,000**

This yellow chair by British designer Mark Robson (b.1965) is one of his early pieces made from the new GRP (glass-reinforced polyester). Growing environmental awareness and concerns about the finite life of our natural resources encouraged fresh young designers like Robson to look at a new generation of plastics. These took less energy and fossil fuel to make than traditional materials and they were sure to have a longer life. Robson took advantage of GRP's flexibility and strength, and came up with a functional design that could easily be mass produced. Collectors value this chair for its modern solution to a contemporary problem. **£2,500-3,500**

An estimated 1,000 million across the world witnessed, via TV and radio, the fairy tale marriage of HRH Prince Charles, Prince of Wales and Lady Diana Spencer at St Paul's Cathedral on 29 July 1981. The couple's engagement, officially announced on 24 February, gave commemorative manufacturers plenty of time to get into production and make sure that nearly every household item (from biscuit tins to playing cards) in some way marked the royal wedding. This unopened tin of Sharps mini mints was at the bottom end of the commemorative market. The tragic death of Diana, Princess of Wales on 31 August 1997 has even added a premium to humble commemoratives like this associated with key aspects of her life. **£6**

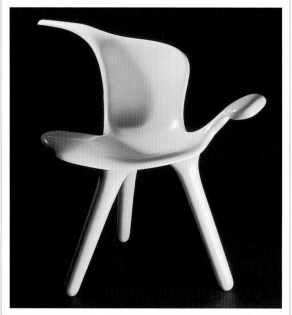

This brightly coloured 'Super' table or floor lamp seems to have a life of its own. Its French designer, Martine Bedin, was a member of the influential Memphis Group, formed by Ettore Sottsass and a band of progressive new designers in Italy in 1980. Memphis aimed to find a totally new vision of design that was less elitist and far less academic than anything before. In a way, Bedine's hedgehog form poked fun at the grand visual references the Modernists made. It also took household lighting into a new dimension – it shed light on your room but it also brightened up your life too. Like any 'pet', 'Super' was your companion, there to welcome you home at the end of the day! Memphis designs are avidly collected because of their ground-breaking style. Their rarity lies in limited production runs that were never cheap. A metal label giving the designer's details and the year it was made points to an authentic piece. **£630**

DANNY LANE TABLE

Taking industrial glass and transforming it into daring sculptural furniture is the key to American glass artist Danny Lane's (b. 1955) designs. In 1981 he set up his first London studio and this console table is an early use of his slab technique. Against a backdrop of vast warehouse-style eighties space, glass furniture worked brilliantly, and Lane's stacked table legs had a real sense of flow as well as being intriguingly translucent. He also conveyed a feeling of fluidity and movement by placing an irregularly shaped piece of glass on top for the tabletop. With a string of awards behind him and pieces around the world in private and public collections (including his specially commissioned mezzanine balustrade at London's Victoria and Albert Museum, 1994), Danny Lane is a modern master. His one-off originals, which tend to carry his signature, as well as his limited edition runs change hands for thousands at auction. **£5,000+ (specially commissioned pieces)**

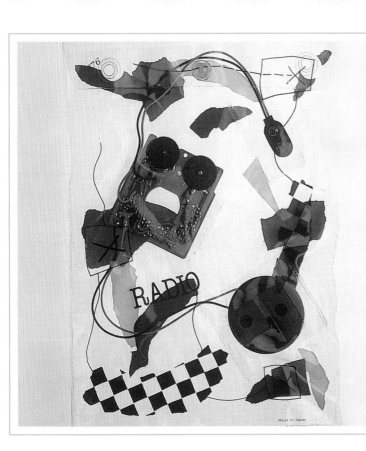

BAG RADIO

In a world that saw Hi-fi shrink even further thanks to innovations like Sony's Walkman (1979), Royal College of Art graduate, Daniel Weil (b. 1953) took radio portability, presentation and size into a new dimension with this 'Bag Radio' (1981). His intention was to create 'a new imagery for electronics to escape from the mechanical imagery of the box'. What he came up with was totally novel – a radio whose workings you could see and feel through a screen-printed PVC plastic envelope. British firm Parenthesis made Weil's design commercially and originals (as opposed to cheap Far Eastern copies) were stamped '© D WEIL 1981' on the lower edge. All you needed were two AA batteries to pick up the hit sounds of your choice. And as you can imagine novelty meant that it was used and shown to friends, so relatively few classic 'Bag Radios' have survived. **£100-150**

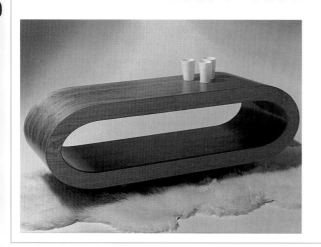

Side tables are still very much a part of today's sitting room. British designer, Lynne Wilson, played with streamlined simplicity with her 'Loopy Table' (1997), which was inspired by a visit to the laundrette. 'I was loading up the washing machine and thought, what beautiful shapes,' she says. After a series of sketches, the squashed Polo-mint-looking 'Loopy', under the 'Budgie Designs' label, was born. Technically, the 'Loopy Table' may be difficult to make from MDF (medium density fibreboard), but already it's caught the eye of the government (who selected it for the European Summit Meeting, 1997), advertisers (who featured it in McDonald's and Mars commercials) and the Victoria and Albert Museum, who have a section devoted to 'Loopy' in their archives. **£660**

The clean white lines and simplicity of this 'Magazine' sofa were considered just the thing to relax the assembled gathering of prime ministers and presidents at London's Anglo-French summit (1997). Michael Young's low-level design (the first to come out of his newly formed MY022 company), was styled specifically for Japanese interiors and was 'the result' he says 'of me playing with different shapes'. But it soon became a comfortable favourite in the West after heads of state had used it for chatting. A run of chairs and tables in the same style is also part of Young's successful 'Magazine' range. Early issues in pure, uncomplicated white have been augmented by coloured versions, now available in Japan. **£2,600**

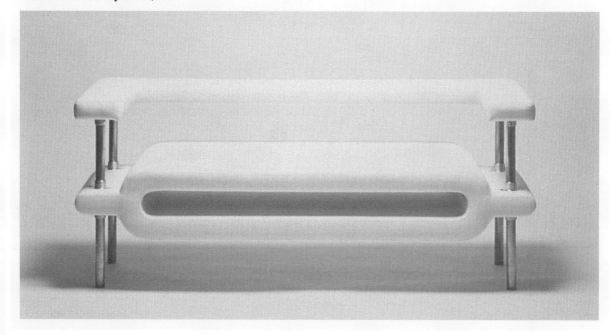

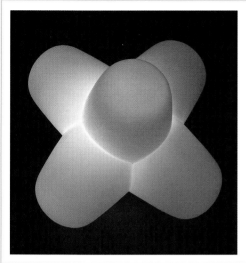

'JACK'

Cheap and certainly cheerful, Tom Dixon's 'Jack' for Eurolounge (1996) is whatever you want it to be. In tune with other nineties designs, it's the home owner who dictates just what role his possessions take in the sitting room! As British designer Dixon (b. 1959) says, 'it's a sitting, lighting, stacking thing,' there to serve any number of functions in a new way. Basically it's a play on the traditional children's game of 'jacks', meaning you've got six 'legs', which gives you extraordinary stability and flexibility. Whichever way up, three will always remain in contact with the ground. This one is white but the plastic shell with a light inside also comes in seven other colours including a dramatic fluorescent version. Dixon is a guru of modern British design who was plucked in 1998 to head the design team at Habitat. The 'Jack' itself was earmarked as a key piece of 'Cool Britannia' at London's influential Powerhouse::UK Exhibition (1998). **£165**

'DINO' TABLE

Versatility is also the key to this 'Dino' table-cum-chair-cum-stool-cum-sculpture! It's part of a 'Design to Communicate' collection made by talented British collective Jam (founded 1994) for leading foam manufacturer Zotefoams PLC. Jam rose to the challenge of finding a new market for a packaging and medical material – their aim being to carve out a niche for Zotefoam in the home. When the multifunctional 'Dino' arrived in a blaze of publicity at London's Selfridges department store, it was hailed as quirky and original. Plus it showed just how versatile both the foam and the 'Dino' could be. **£828**

'BALZAC' ARMCHAIR AND OTTOMAN

The 'Balzac' armchair and ottoman by British designer Matthew Hilton (b.1957) is 'slump down' comfort at its best. Once you've taken the plunge and paid that little bit extra for this great piece of design, you won't ever want to get up again! It's made by modern furniture makers SCP (founded in London in 1985) and like much of Hilton's work reflects his concern for the social context that his pieces are placed in. Design, for him, should be more than skin deep. His furniture is there to perform a much needed role in the home and it must meet that brief by, amongst other things, being comfortable. Since the 'Balzac' was unveiled at the Milan Furniture Show in 1997 private collectors have scooped it up and just last year it was chosen as a key piece for the nineties room at London's Geffrye Museum. **£1,794 (chair) £634 (ottoman)**

'CHROMAWALL'

With a background in designing electronics for seventies' discos, you can see where British designer Jeremy Lord (b.1950) is coming from with his 'Chromawall'. Fitting for the nineties – a decade that's steeped in retro – where we're used to seeing psychedelic colours at every turn, Lord takes us one step further. This is a moving mosaic experience that's designed to enliven our lives and our living rooms. Within an aluminium frame are nine plastic modules, each measuring forty-three centimetres across. These modules are arranged into four slightly domed sections, behind these are four coloured lamps that light up in pre-programmed sequences – a visual spectacle that's got a feeling of the circus about it. In this performance though, the colours softly blend in an unexpected way – it's mesmerising and, as Lord says, 'challenges our comprehension'. When it was unveiled at Britain's '100% Design' show (1995) the 'Chromawall' (now manufactured by Ward's Colour Light Company est. 1994), was an instant hit. Leading lights from the world of pop; Damon Albarn of British band Blur and Icelandic singer Björk, have already snapped up one each and so too has the Museum of Contemporary Art in Los Angeles. With other equally novel and diverse designs in the pipeline Jeremy Lord and 'Chromawall' can only go far. **£5,000**

GELLO TABLE

Side tables are still very much a part of today's living rooms but as you can see from this approach there's no binding style – only a thread of flexibility running through each. The concertina 'Gello' table (1994) by Australian designer Marc Newson (b.1963) for the French store Les Trois Suisses, uses plastic in an innovative way. Its honeycomb base may look rather like a Christmas decoration but, says Newson, the shape is actually based on Chinese paper lanterns. The see-through plastic (in a variety of funky colours), is actually surprisingly strong and featherlight when it's fused like this. The fact that production ceased in 1997 adds to its collectability. **£100**

Tragedy struck Britain's Royal Family with the premature death of Diana Princess of Wales on 31 August 1997. To the millions around the world who watched with sadness as the funeral cortège slowly made its way from her home at Kensington Palace to Westminster Abbey, Diana was a true 'Queen of Hearts'. In life she spawned a loyal following and quality mementoes marking her marriage to HRH Prince Charles, Prince of Wales in 1981 and the birth of the two Royal Princes, William and Harry, were sought after by collectors. Only a few months before her death a Christie's auction of Diana's dresses raised over £1.9 million for charity. However, after 31 August, things changed dramatically and interest in anything 'Diana' became insatiable. This limited edition copy of the 'Dresses' catalogue (one of 250) from the charity auction, that originally sold for £1,250 in June 1997, was valued at £25,000-30,000 little more than a year later. However, the key to any commemorative relating to the Princess is quality. This mug is one of very few fine pieces made to commemorate her death. Commissioned by Carlins Collectables it was issued in a limited run of 100 and each mug is individually numbered. It's important to look for items where the transfer-printed lettering (detailing the key episodes in her life) and the image of the Princess are well reproduced.

£25,000-35,000 ('Dresses' auction catalogue) £15-20 (Diana mug)

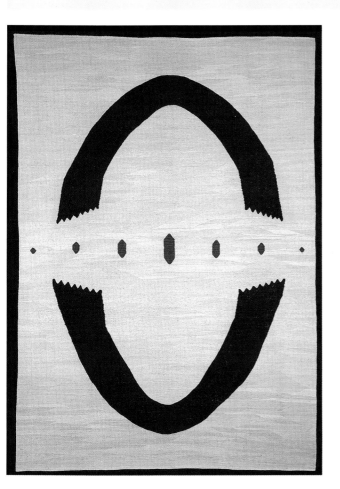

The traditional art of rug-weaving has taken on a nineties look with Christopher Farr's (b.1953) 'Shell' rug from his 'Flint' collection (1997). 'I was really trying to do something that was quite modern and contemporary,' he explains. By embracing the shapes that appear around us in today's furniture and nature, Farr has put the stamp of the nineties on his work. For collectors, there's the comforting thought that not everybody will own something this special. Each rug is laboriously flat woven by hand and only fifteen of these have been made.
£2,900

ALESSI
The Italian design company, Alessi, was founded in 1921, when Giovanni Alessi Anghini set up a plate turning workshop with a foundry at Bagnella in Omegna. This firm specializes in styling kitchen and household products in a highly innovative way. Top designers are a key part of the Alessi look and new lines are recognizable by their bright colours and individual style.

APPLE
Apple Computer Inc. grew out of Steven Wozniak and Steven Jobs's Apple I computer in 1976. But the American firm didn't really take off until 1977, when their Apple II ignited the computer revolution and the PC market. In 1984 Apple introduced the ground-breaking Mackintosh and since then, they have launched a range of innovative products. In 1998 the firm launched the iMac which has become the most popular computer in America.

BAYGEN
The South African, Baygen Power Company Limited, was formed in 1994 to further the wind-up radio concept pioneered by British inventor, Trevor Baylis. Their first product, the Baygen Freeplay radio, built primarily for use in the developing world, was launched in January 1996. Since then it has won countless design awards. Their most recent product is the self-powered everlasting torch (1998).

BESWICK
The Beswick pottery was established in Staffordshire by James Wright Beswick in 1894. In 1947 the firm produced the first in an enduring series of Beatrix Potter models. The company was taken over by Royal Doulton in 1969 and today produces a range of character jugs and figures.

BODUM
Founded in 1944, the Danish family-owned company launched their first product, the Santos coffee maker, in 1958. In 1986 they opened their first shop in London. Their design company, Pi Design AG, located in Switzerland, styles their diverse range of household products. Their maxim, which still holds true today, is that good design should not be expensive.

BRAUN
This mighty appliance manufacturer was founded in 1921 by Max Braun in Frankfurt, Germany. Initially Braun made components for the radio industry before turning their attention to full-scale equipment. They were the first company to combine a radio with a record player. Using a team of skilled product designers, including Dieter Rams and G.A Muller, Braun gained mass recognition in the fifties and sixties for their technical excellence combined with innovative clean-cut design. In 1967 the Gillette Company became the majority shareholder in Braun.

CARLTON WARE
Staffordshire ceramics firm, Carlton Ware, grew out of the Wiltshaw & Robinson pottery that was founded in 1890. They're renowned for their enormous variety of patterns, shapes and glazes, which were always sought after. Family owned for 75 years, the firm was sold in 1987 and the name is still used today.

DECCA
This record company first began in England when stockbroker Edward Lewis formed the Decca Record Company, Ltd. The name was derived from the Deccan Plateau, which was a source of shellac used in phonograph records. In 1934, the American Decca Recording Company was formed and Decca became one of America's most illustrious record labels. The company is controlled by MCA Records today.

DENBY
The great Derbyshire pottery, Denby, dates back to 1809 and it made its name with classic salt-glazed stoneware bottles. Denby tableware was a natural development, as the stoneware could cope with the intense heat of a range and also be transferred to the table. As the versatility and resilience of Denby was appreciated the firm expanded. During the twenties and thirties they branched into decorative art pottery with striking coloured glazes. Their post-war 'Cheviot' and 'Greenwheat' ranges typify the fifties, and Arabesque the sixties. The diversity that has run throughout Denby's history remains a key part of the firm today.

DYSON
James Dyson struck out on his own in 1974 to develop his award winning 'Ballbarrow' an innovative new wheelbarrow. In 1993, he launched the revolutionary Dyson DC01 upright vacuum cleaner in the UK, which was followed the same year by a cylinder model, the DC02- the world's first bag-less cylinder vacuum cleaner. His inventions have won some twenty major design awards and James Dyson has become one of Britain's most successful designers. In 1999 he was elected Chairman of the Design Museum.

ELECTROLUX
In 1912 Axel Wenner-Gren invented the world's first vacuum cleaner - the Lux 1 in Stockholm. Electrolux was subsequently born out of the merger between Elektromekaniska and Lux in 1919. The new firm expanded into other domestic gadgets and in 1925 marketed their first refrigerator - the 'D-fridge'. The fifties saw their manufacture of the first household washing machine followed by a chest freezer and dishwasher. Today, Electrolux is a world leader in household appliances.

FORMICA
Founded in 1913 in Ohio, the Formica Corporation is a recognized innovator in the surfacing industry. The first British factory opened in 1947 selling decorative laminate. It made modern furnishing possible because it was durable, easy to clean and came in a palette of colours and patterns. In 1995 the firm was acquired by Australia-based BTR Nylex.

G-PLAN
In 1895, Ebenezer Gomme started a chair workshop in Buckinghamshire. Between the wars, Gomme's was the first to introduce the idea of the dining room suite. The innovative G-Plan furniture range (from 1953) appealed to the public for decades. In 1992 the High Wycombe factory closed. Today upholstered G-Plan furniture is made in Wiltshire while G-Plan cabinet-making continues in Glasgow.

GOBLIN
The first Goblin Teasmade was invented by Brenner Thornton in 1936. It was an automatic electric tea maker developed by the British Vacuum Cleaner company. Today Goblin is part of the Glen Dimplex Group.

GUZZINI
This Italian firm started in the 1900s designing items of cutlery using ox horn. In the fifties and sixties Guzzini made plastic tableware in two-tone colour ranges. Today they are a market leader in household styling and design.

HABITAT
Terence Conran founded habitat in 1964 with the aim of selling well-designed contemporary housewares and home furnishings. The first store opened in Fulham Road, London, with a stock of 2000 practical furnishing items and a completely fresh approach to furniture retailing. Habitat is now an international retailing company specialising in contemporary housewares and home furnishings with a theme of stylish but practical design.

HASBRO
Hasbro was founded in 1923 in America by two brothers, Henry and Helal Hassenfield. Toy successes included Mr Potato Head (1950s) and GI Joe (1964). In 1991, they acquired Kenner Products who make Star Wars toys and in 1993 Hasbro reintroduced Action Man to the modern toy market.

HERMAN MILLER
American furniture giant, Herman Miller, was founded in 1923 to further modern designed furniture by designers such as Eero Saarinen, George Nelson and Charles Eames The company produced some of the most successful functional designs of the early post-war period e.g. Eames' one-piece moulded DAR chair in 1948.

HOOVER
Hoover was founded in Ohio, USA, in 1908. The first British factory opened at Perivale, Middlesex in 1932, to produce upright cleaners and the firm quickly became the established leader in the floor care market. Today Hoover sells over two million domestic appliances every year.

HORNSEA
In 1949 brothers Desmond and Colin Rawson started the Hornsea pottery on Yorkshire's east coast. One of their key designers was John Clapisson who styled the 'Home Décor' range in the late fifties and 'Studiocraft' in the sixties. After several changes of ownership, Hornsea is once again privately owned and is Britain's largest 'studio' pottery supplying Harrods, BHS and Boots.

JVC
The Victor Company of Japan (JVC) was founded in 1927 as a manufacturer of records and phonographs. After countless breakthroughs like the VHS format for home use (1976), today, JVC is one of the world's leading electronics giants.

KENWOOD
Kenwood Manufacturing Company Ltd was founded in 1947 by entrepreneur, Kenneth Wood (1916-97). From its humble beginnings next to a fish shop in Woking, Surrey came the firm's first product - an electrical turnover toaster. A year later in 1948 the first all-British food mixer was born and was later sold as The Kenwood Chef. In 1951 the first Kenwood blender - the Kenmix appeared, to be joined by a handmixer (the Chef Minor) in 1952. Kenneth Grange of Pentagram Design Limited was brought in to redesign the Chef in 1960 and his new-look mixer was exported to kitchens world-wide. In 1968 Kenwood became part of Thorn Electrical Industries and in 1989 the firm saw a management buy-out. Three years later it was floated on the London Stock Exchange. Today Kenwood is a global household name.

KNOLL INTERNATIONAL
Hans Knoll, son of a German furniture maker, founded the Hans G. Knoll Furniture Company in 1938, in New York. His philosophy, based on pre-war Bauhaus modernism, was that good design benefits everyone and that modern architectural design needed equally modern furniture. Together with his wife Florence, Knoll gave a new look to interiors by collaborating with leading and up-and-coming architects and designers to create original classic furniture. The tradition continues today with recent designs from Sottsass and Frank Gehry.

LEICA
The first commercially produced Leica camera, the Leica I (a name taken from manufacturer, 'Leitz' and the word 'camera') was introduced in 1925. Successive improvements and the introduction of the revolutionary Leica M3 with bayonet fittings in the fifties sealed the firm's success, contributing to its reputation as one of the all-time camera greats.

LESNEY
British toy maker, Lesney, was founded in 1947 by Leslie and Rodney Smith - hence the name 'Lesney'. In 1953, Lesney Products registered the trademark 'Matchbox', marketing under the Moko company. Lesney Products Corporation was bought out in 1982 and eventually became Matchbox International Ltd.

LOUIS MARX
Nicknamed the 'Toy King of America', Louis Marx established the Louis Marx Toy Company in 1921. It was the first firm to mass-produce mechanical toys in America. And by 1950 the company was the world's largest toy manufacturer.

MATTEL
American toy giant, Mattel, traces its beginnings to 1945. The original founders were Harold Matson and Elliot Handler, who coined ' Mattel' by combining letters of their last and first names respectively. Matson soon sold out to his partner, Elliot, whose wife, Ruth Handler, created the first Barbie doll in 1959. In 1995 Mattel took over production of Cabbage Patch Kids.

MECCANO
This British company was founded by Frank Hornby in 1901. Their Dinky toys were marketed from 1933. In 1964, the company was taken over by Tri-ang and closed in 1979.

MERRYTHOUGHT
This leading British teddy bear firm was founded in 1930 by A. Janisch and C. Rendle. In the fifties and sixties their line of 'Cheeky' bears found mass-market appeal. Merrythought still makes these today as well as a host of other soft toys and teddies.

METTOY

A British toy company founded by Henry Ullmann, which specialized in tinplate toys from the thirties to the fifties. In 1956, Mettoy introduced the first of their famous Corgi toys.

MIDWINTER

Midwinter was founded in 1910 by William R Midwinter. In the fifties his son, Roy Midwinter, brought ideas of contemporary style and design to Britain from America. His 'Stylecraft' tableware (from 1953) was developed for the mass market. In-house designer, Jessie Tait, styled a range of designs as did the young Terence Conran, Hugh Casson and Peter Scott. The Midwinter factory closed in 1987.

MOORCROFT

William Moorcroft worked as an artist potter for the Staffordshire firm of James Macintyre & Co. from 1898. With the backing of the Liberty family (he married the retailer's daughter), Moorcroft set up his own pottery in 1913 at Cobridge. Today a talented team of in-house designers follow in his footsteps, producing a range of highly collectable modern wares under the Moorcroft banner.

MORPHY RICHARDS

In 1935 Donal Morphy and Charles Richards joined forces, and started the British company, Morphy Richards, a year later. They aimed to give all housewives affordable electrical appliances. In 1947, Morphy Richards became a public company and today the firm is part of the Glen Dimplex Group.

NUTBROWN

This kitchenware maker, named after its founder Thomas M. Nutbrown, began in Blackpool in 1927 and closed in 1988. Products included baking utensils such as novelty biscuit cutters. Nutbrown products are now made by Fiskars UK Ltd.

OLIVETTI

On his return from a trip to the United States, in 1908, Camillo Olivetti formed the Olivetti company - Italy's first typewriter factory. In 1911, the M1 was a masterpiece of engineering and further models of typewriters and calculators made Olivetti world famous. Olivetti is now active in the field of telephony and I.T. services.

PANASONIC

This leading Japanese electronics firm grew out of the Matsushita Electric Housewares Manufacturing Works set up by Konosuke Matsushita in 1918. Panasonic set up in the UK in 1972.

PEDIGREE

The name Pedigree was first registered in 1942. Pedigree Soft Toys Ltd. was a subsidiary of Lines Bros. Ltd. From 1937 the company started to produce a range of soft toys. One of their great successes was Sindy who first appeared in 1963.

PIFCO

Pifco (The Provincial Incandescent Fitting Company) was founded in 1900 by British entrepreneur Joseph Webber. They initially specialized in lighting before becoming a leader in household electrical products, which they still manufacture today.

POLAROID

The Polaroid Corporation was formed in 1937 in Boston USA, to further develop the light polarising material called 'polaroid', invented by Edwin H Land some years earlier. As well as polarising films and plastics, the firm was famed for its one-step photographic system and cameras.

POOLE

Based in Poole, Dorset, the Poole pottery began life in 1873 under the name of Dorset tile company. Carter & Co. In 1921 it expanded to become Carter, Stabler & Adams, producing tableware and a range of simply shaped, colourful vases. The firm did not officially trade as 'Poole' until 1963, although 'Poole England' was added to the backstamp in the fifties. Today the firm is very much a thriving concern.

PSION

Psion was founded in the UK in 1980 by its chairman, David Potter. With the launch of the Psion Organiser in 1984, Psion became the world's first volume manufacturer of handheld computing products. The latest Series 5 model has been acknowledged as delivering unparalleled computing power inside an innovative product design. Chosen by the UK Design Council as a 'Millennium Product', it has also won a number of international awards, and is sold world-wide.

PULSAR

In 1972 the Hamilton Watch Company launched the first digital watch - the 'Pulsar' in America which spawned a revolution in time keeping. Today the firm, known as Pulsar, is a major brand in Western Europe.

PYREX

Originally developed for American railroad lanterns in 1912 by the Corning Glass Works, USA, Pyrex glass (as it was known from 1915) was revolutionary. It was resistant to heat and temperature change making it ideal for both baking and serving. In 1922, James A. Jobling, a Newcastle businessman acquired the license to make Pyrex in Britain. Initially Pyrex 'oven glassware' was clear but early Flameware (made from 1936 in the USA) had a bluish tone. Coloured (opal) Pyrex was introduced to America in 1947 and came to Britain shortly after to fit with 'gay' fifties kitchens. British Pyrex carries the distinctive James A. Jobling (JAJ) shield. American Pyrex is usually clearly marked 'made in the USA'.

RACE FURNITURE LIMITED

In partnership with Noel Jordan, designer Ernest Race (1913-64) started the British firm in London's Clapham, producing a range of original and forward-looking furniture, just after the War. In 1951 the famous 'Antelope' chair made for 'The Festival of Britain' was put on show. A comparatively high price tag put a number of the firm's designs beyond the average pocket and many were bought for office use.

ROBOT COUPE

In 1960 Frenchman, Pierre Verdun, set up his own company, Robot Coupe, which by the late sixties had produced the world's first real food processor for the catering trade - the R2. In 1972, their first domestic product, the Magimix, was made for food preparation tasks still only done by hand in the home. It was launched in the UK in 1974 and updated models are available today.

RUSSELL HOBBS

In 1952 William Russell and Peter Hobbs left Morphy Richards. Shortly afterwards they set up British electrical giant, Russell Hobbs. In 1955, they produced the design classic the K1 kettle. Today they are best known for their innovative Millennium Kettle. The firm is now part of the Pifco Group.

SINCLAIR

The British firm Sinclair Radionics was set up in 1961 by Clive Sinclair. After introducing a range of well-designed and pioneering electronic products that included watches and the world's first pocket calculator, Sinclair launched the Sinclair ZX80 - the world's smallest and cheapest computer in 1980. It used a domestic television set as a screen and a cassette player as a program and data store. It was swiftly followed by the hugely successful ZX81. 1982 saw the launch of the ZX Spectrum.

SPODE

One of Britain's leading Staffordshire ceramics factories founded by Josiah Spode in 1770. In the 19th century they became famous for their bone china tableware, which is internationally renowned today.

SUNBEAM

Sunbeam was founded in Chicago in 1897 by John K. Stewart and Thomas J. Clark to manufacture mechanical horse clippers. Its first electrical appliance, an electric iron, was produced in 1910. The company soon became a major manufacturer of innovative portable appliances and electric consumer goods. In 1946 the firm became the Sunbeam Corporation. Its products are still sold worldwide today.

SUSIE COOPER

Susie Cooper studied textile and fashion design at Burslem, Staffordshire in 1922. In 1929, with her brother-in-law, Jack Beeson, she set up independently at the George Street Pottery, Tunstall. Much of her inspiration came from nature - many of her patterns have floral names. In 1966 Wedgwood took over the pottery. She continued as a ceramics designer until her death in 1995.

SWATCH

Although the Swatch trade name was formally established in 1981, the origins of the Swiss brand go back to the late seventies, when the technology for an inexpensive quartz watch was developed. They introduced their Swatch wristwatch in 1983 and were the first brand to make watches a stylish fashion accessory. The first major Swatch auction was held by Sotheby's in 1990, elevating the watches to the status of art objects. Two years later the first Swatch Store in the UK opened, swiftly followed by the UK arm of the Swatch Collectors' Club. Swatch Telecom took the firm into telecommunications with products like the Swatch cordless DECT telephone (launched in 1997).

T. G. GREEN

British ceramics firm, T.G. Green, began in Church Gresley, Derbyshire in 1864. From the solid mocha-decorated jugs of last century to the simulated-tiger print 'Safari' TV-plates from the fifties, T.G. Green (which is still a going concern today under the Cloverleaf banner) made a vast array of dinner, tea and utility wares for nearly every middle class home. They are best known for blue and white banded Cornish Ware, launched 1926 and redesigned in 1967.

THERMOS

Thermos Ltd was registered as a UK brand in 1907 after the first company to manufacture vacuum flasks for commercial use had formed in Germany in 1904 (Thermos GmbH). The firm produced a hugely successful line of glass vacuum flasks with immense heat-saving ability.

TRI-ANG

Tri-ang Toys, an offshoot of the flourishing British toymakers, Lines Bors. Ltd. was established in 1919. The Tri-ang triangular trademark was registered in 1927 and the firm dominated English tinplate production.

VENINI

The Italian firm of Vetri Soffiati Cappelin, Venini & C. was founded in 1921 by two driving forces, Venetian antique dealer Giacomo Cappellin and lawyer Paolo Venini who managed the firm. Many artists and designers collaborated with Venini and in the fifties foreign designers such as Tapio Wirkkala were taken on board. After changing hands, the firm became Venini Spa in 1988.

VILLEROY & BOCH

In 1748, together with his sons, Francois Boch began manufacturing ceramics in Germany. From a small pottery in Audun-le-Tiche, the family firm is a global concern today producing some of the finest tableware on the market.

VOGUE

Vogue was a fashion magazine produced by Condé Nast. First seen in 1892 in America, Britain in 1916 and France in the twenties, Vogue became a publication whose influence in the international world of high fashion was unparalleled. The growth of the Vogue Pattern Service (est. 1905) gave women a chance to wear Paris couture style, duplicated in pattern form.

WADE

Wade pottery was founded in 1810 in Stoke-on-Trent and today is known as The Wade Ceramics Group. One of their most successful lines was their miniature animal series, named Whimsies, popular from 1954. Wade also made the successful run of piggy banks for the Nat West bank promotion in the eighties.

WEDGWOOD

Josiah Wedgwood founded this own pottery in 1759 at Burslem, Staffordshire. By the late 18th century it was known for its cream-coloured earthenware or creamware. Today the ceramics giant has achieved international success thanks to its bone china tableware.

ACKNOWLEDGEMENTS

KEY: t=top; b=bottom; c=centre; l=left; r=right

PHOTOGRAPHERS
AW = Andy Woods (© Andy Woods Photography)
DI = © David Irving
HCW = Harry Cory-Wright
PW = Peter Woods
RD = Roger Dixon (© André Deutsch)

RF= © Robert Fairer
Roy = Roy Farthing at The 20th Century Show, Chelsea
SS = © Steve Shipman
TG = © Tim Griffiths
TH = Terry Hefferma

COLLECTIONS, MUSEUMS & WHERE TO BUY
A = Alfies Antiques Market London (0171 723 6066)
B = Bonhams auctioneers (0171 393 3900)
Books for Cooks (0171 221 1992)
BM = Bookmark, children's books (01793 731693)
Bridgewater Pottery Limited (0171 371 9033)
CB = Christina Bishop Kitchenware (0171 435 1959)
Century Design –US modern specialists (0171 4875100)
CF= Christopher Farr Handmade Rugs (0171 792 5761)
CG = Clarke Gammon auctioneers (01483 880915)
CK = Colin Kostyrka
Conran Shop (0171 589 7401)
Corning Museum of Glass, USA (001 607 974 8257)
CSK = Christie's Auctioneers (0171 581 7611)
D = Denby China Matching (01234 771745)
David Mellor (0171 730 4259)
Design Museum London (0171 403 6933)
DL= Danny Lane (0181 968 3399)
FA = The Fine Art Society Plc, C20th design (0171 629 5116)
FB = Frances Baird
FD = Flying Duck Enterprises, fifties to seventies specialists
    (0181 858 1964)
Festival, fifties to seventies specialists (0181 840 9333)
Glass Museum on line (www.glass.co.nz)
HG = Hope & Glory Commemoratives (0171 727 8424)
HOA = Huxtables Old Advertising (0171 724 2200)
KB = Kitchen Bygones (0171 258 3405 – at Alfies)
Lulu Guinness (0171 221 9686)
M = W. Moorcroft PLC (01782 214323)
Mid = Midwinter China Matching (0181 572 4328)
Museum of Advertising and Packaging (01452 302309)

Museum of the Moving Image (0171 815 1331)
P = Phillips auctioneers (0171 629 6602)
Pc = Private Collection
Philip Treacy Ltd (0171 259 9605)
Portsmouth City Museum, period room sets (01705 827261)
Ray = Ray Richardson
Richard Dennis Gallery – pre/post-war ceramics (0171 7272061)
RR = Retro Rentals, fifties–eighties fashion hire (0173 690850)
Ruth Warner perfume collection (by appointment (01233 636185)
S = Sotheby's auctioneers (0171 493 8080)
Science Museum, London – 'The Secret Life of the Home'
    Gallery (0171 938 8008)
StC = St. Clere Antiques Carlton Ware Specialists
    (01474 853630)
SC = Susie Cooper Ceramics (0171 723 0449)
SCP = SCP Ltd – contemporary furniture (0171 739 1869)
SK = Skinner Inc., Boston MA, auctioneers (001 617 350 5400)
SP = Scotia Phonecards (www.scotiaphonecards.mcmail.com)
SPA = Space – contemporary design (0171 229 6533)
SSO = Simply Switch On – virtual gadget museum
    (www.westworld.dmu.ac.uk/electricity/sso.html)
T = Target Gallery – modern design (0171 636 6295)
TC =Telephone Card Catalogue Company (Fax: 0181 651 6390)
Timney Fowler Ltd (0171 352 2263)
V = Viaduct Furniture Ltd – modern furniture (0171 278 8456)
VWM = Vintage Wireless Museum
VWC = Vintage Wireless Company, Dulwich (0161 973 0438)
Wycombe Museum (for G-Plan) (01494 421895)
20-21 = TwentyTwentyOne – modern design (0171 288 1996)

CREDITS
Front Cover Tl & 30 bl John Merkle/ Ecko Housewares Inc. tc & 44bl RD/B, tr & 112b AW/20-21, bl & 146tr AW/Pc, bc & 153b SCP, br & 93b RD/B, Back Cover, tl & 62b CSK, tr & 114t RD/HOA, bl, 3 & 81t CSK, bc & 12b RD/KB, br & 87b RD/CSK, Front flap M, Back flap SS

1 & 43b RD/SC, 8 & 12c RD/CB, 10t RD/SSO, b RD/Pc, 11 ©Kenwood Appliances plc, 12t RD/KB, 13tl RD/HOA, tr RD/HG, b RD/Pc, 14t RD/CB, c RD/SSO, b RD/KB, 15t RD/SSO, bl & r RD/T, 16 ©Pentagram Design Limited, 17t RD/T, b RD/Pc, 18t RD/HOA, bl & r RD/Pc, 19cl &bl RD/Pc, cr RD/T, 20 Pc, 21t & bl RD/FD, cr RD/HOA, br S, 22tl RD/FD, tr RD/B, b RD/Pc, 23t RD/FD, b RD/CB, 24t © Pi Design AG, Luzern, Switzerland, b RD/CB, 25t RD/CB, b © W&T Avery Limited, 26t © Alessi Spa Italy, b RD/CB, 27t © SeymourPowell, b RD/CB, 28t © Dyson, b © Duchy Originals Limited, 29t © Inflate, c © Russell Hobbs, b ©Alessi Spa Italy, 30br ©Guzzini, 31t © Electrolux, c RD/Giftware International, b Mitchell Beazley, 33 & 44br RD/B, 35t RD/D, b RD/SC, 36tl & tr RD/FD, b RD/Mid, 37t RD/D, b RD/T 38cl RD/B, cr RD/Pc, b RD/StC, 39t S, b RD/Pc, 40t CSK, b The Fine Art Society/The Target Gallery London, 41t RD/D, b RD/Mid, 42cl & bl RD/Pc, br CSK, 43t RD/B, 44t RD/B, 45 RD/B, 46t RD/T, bl RD/B, br RD/Mid, 47cl RD/D, cr ©The Philadelphia Museum of Art: Gift of Janet Kerr, b CSK 48t & b RD/StC, 49t RD/Mid, b S 50cl ©Knoll, cr RD/StC, b M, 51t S, b ©Villeroy & Boch, 52t ©Smart Design, b B, 53t Philip Vile/©Branson Coates, b HCW/©Bridgewater Pottery Ltd, 54cl ©David Mellor, cl RD/©Conran Design Partnership, b ©Emma O'Dare, 55t CSK, b V, 56 cl ©Transglass, cr ©Fenella Mallelieu, b M, 58 ©The Pifco Group, 60t P, b CSK, 61t RD/Pc, b RD/HOA, 62cl T, cr RD/SSO, 63tr S, cl CSK, b RD/T, 64t CSK, b RD/HOA, 65tr & bl S, 66t RD/B, b CSK, 67tl & tr CSK, 68tl RD/FD, cr S, bl RD/B, 69 S, 70tr CSK, cl RD/RR, br CSK, 71 RD/RR, 72tr S, bl CSK, 73t B, b RD/RR, 74tl RD/RR, br S, 75©Swatch, 76b CSK, 77tl RD/RR, cr RD/RR, bl ©Press Association, 78b ©Wallpaper-Time Inc, 79 SCP, 80t TG, bl RF, 81bl ©Lulu Guinness, br ©Farah Lister, 83 CSK, 85t CSK, b RD/B, 86 RD/FB, b CSK, 87t CSK, b RD/FD, 89tl RD/BM, b RD/Pc, b CSK, 90t RD/B, c RD/BM, b S, 91t RD/FB, b RD/B, 92t & c RD/B, b CSK, 93tl S, tr CSK, 94t RD/B, c CSK, b RD/BM, 96t RD/FD, b P, 97t CSK, b RD/FD, 98 RD/B, 99t B, b ©Wade Ceramics, 100t RD/BM, b RD/FD, 101t DI/Ray, b RD/B, 102t RD/RR, b RD/B, 103t & b RD/B, 104t RD/CSK, b Pc, 105t ©Jane Atfield, b RD/B, 106t ©Dorling Kindersley Limited, b S, 108 & 125b RD/CK, 110t RD/B, b B, 111t CSK, b RD/Pc, 112t CSK, 113 & 114b CSK, 115 S, 116t RD/B, b RD/FD, 117tl CSK, tr RD/FD, b ©Polaroid Corporate Archives, 118t S, c S, bl RD/FD, br CSK, 119tl RD/B, tr RD/HOA, b S, 120 & 121t & b RD/B, 122t B, bl S, br RD/Pc, 123t ©The Computer Museum History Center, CA, b CSK, 124t TC, b RD/CK, 125t Konica, bl & br RD/CK, 126t RD/CK, b ©Lisa Krohn with Tucker Viemeister, 127 BT Museum, 128t Swatch Telecom, b RD/Pc, 129t Alessi Spa Italy, b Knoll International, 130t ©TH/ Apple Computer Inc., b Psion Computers, 131t The Crafts Council, b ©The Baygen Power Company, 133 & 138b RD/HOA, 135t RF/T, bl RD/B, br CSK (both), 136t Roy/T, bl T, br ©FA & T, 137t RD/FD, b RD/HG, 138t RD/B, 139t RD/VWM, b RD/VWM, 140t RD/B, b ©FA & T, 141t RD/VWM, b SK, 142t CSK, bl RD/B, br CSK, 143t RD/HG, b CSK, 144 RD/B, 145tl B, tr CSK, b AW/Pc, 146l B, br RD/HG, 147 CSK, 148 RD/B, 149t RD/HG, b B, 150tl B, tr RD/HOA, b CSK, 151t PW/DL, b ©Pentagram Design Ltd., 152 RD/B, 153t SPA, c Jam, 154t SPA, b '3 Suisses'/Marc Newson, 155t RD/CG, b CF

The author and publisher would like to thank the following: Daniel Agnew, Sarah Allen, Joan & Bob Anderson, Tanya Avetoomyan, Frances Baird, Abigail Baker, Christina Bishop, Richard Chamberlain, Michael Curtis, Roger Dixon, Hugh Edwards, Sue & Bruce Edwards, Anne & Leonora Excell, Fiona Gateley, Hannah Goring, Kenneth Grange, David Huxtable, Neil Johanssen, Nick Jones, Diane Kenyon, Colin Kostyrka, Paul Linnell, Farah Lister, Helen & Keith Martin, David Mellor, Nik Oakley, Alexander Payne, Fred Peskett, Jill Potterton, Dick Powell, Michael Pritchard, Geoffrey Rayner, Claire Richardson, Veronica Roche, John Sharp, Carolyn Shrosbee, Freya Simms, Simon Smith, Emma Sully, Richard Tayler, Suzanne Trisk, Harry Trowell, Ruth Warner, Gerald Wells.